MICHAEL SAVAGE

the political zoo

P9-DFX-338

Published by
THOMAS NELSON
Since 1798

www.thomasnelson.com

*"The true end of satire is the amendment of vice by correction.
And he who writes honestly is no more an enemy to the
offender, than the physician to the patient, when he prescribes
harsh remedies to an inveterate disease. . . ."*

—JOHN DRYDEN, 1681

Copyright © 2006 by Michael A. Weiner, Ph.D.

Illustrations by Dan Brawner [BrawnerArt.com]

Design by Karen Williams [intudesign.net]

All rights reserved. No portion of this book may be reproduced, stored in a retrieval system,
or transmitted in any form or by any means—electronic, mechanical, photocopy, recording,
scanning, or other—except for brief quotations in critical reviews or articles, without the
prior written permission of the publisher.

Published in Nashville, Tennessee, by Thomas Nelson, Inc.

Thomas Nelson, Inc. titles may be purchased in bulk for educational, business, fundraising, or
sales promotional use. For information, please e-mail SpecialMarkets@thomasnelson.com.

Library of Congress cataloging-in-publication data on file with the Library of Congress.

ISBN 1-59555-072-0 / 978-1-59555-072-9

Printed in the United States of America

07 08 09 10 11 RRD 5 4 3 2 1

New Preface

The Political Zoo was eerily ahead of its time. As you can see by the 2006 mid-term elections, people saw through the pretenses and posturing of the Republicrat Party. The fake conservatives lampooned in these pages will have hell to pay from here on. Limbaugh, O'Reilly, Gingrich, Giuliani, McCain, and company have all been given a vote of no confidence.

George W. Bush is, of course, the chief villain. He has destroyed the conservative movement and the Republican Party because of his waffling, war, and weaknesses as a leader.

When you analyze the two parties, the Republicans are actually more liberal than the Democrats on many key issues. Just take the growth of government spending. It's increased at a faster rate under Bush than it did under Clinton! Liberal Bill grew federal spending at an annualized rate of 3.6 percent, but Bush gave us an annualized growth rate of federal spending of 7.3%!

And it doesn't stop there. Bush pushed prescription drug coverage to Medicare recipients, Hillary's wildest dream. He beefed up the Department of Indoctrination—

Education—pushed through CAFTA, is working to create a North American trading zone modeled on the European Union that will further erode our border with Mexico, and, finally, wants to grant amnesty to twenty million illegal aliens.

Big Government Republicans lost the election, not conservatism. Don't forget that. State ballot initiatives saw affirmative action rejected in Michigan, homosexual marriage defeated in four more states, and limits on benefits for illegal aliens even in liberal Arizona.

The Political Zoo warns Americans not to be fooled by labels but to study the actual policies of political animals, all of whom are known by their ability to camouflage their true intentions.

Michael Savage
JANUARY 1, 2007

CoNTeNTS

Intro DucTioN

Welcome to Our Real National Zoo.

Aristotle said, "Man is a political animal." He was right. In ways he could never have imagined. What's more, today's political man is the most bestial of the herd. Just look around. The world of politics is filled with uncivilized, snarling, rapacious beasts that, like untrained mutts, raise their legs and urinate on everything we hold dear. Where have you gone, Rin Tin Tin? Our nation turns its lonely eyes to you.

I scarcely exaggerate. Even my humble dog Teddy behaves better than most political animals. Like just about all dogs, he is loyal. He protects, or at least tries to. He doesn't bite the hand that feeds him. He is man's best friend. Politicians, by and large, are none of the above.

Except for the toga and pederasty, Aristotle would have fit in perfectly in today's political arena. Well, the toga anyhow. He thought government could function best if we all behaved as bees. His ideal society was one in which every citizen-drone served the queen bee, and the queen bee ensured the survival of the hive and governed the issues of life and death with an unquestioned authority. Today's queen "B" Hillary Clinton would love nothing more.

You see, Aristotle had a very low view of the average person. He thought they wouldn't or shouldn't be able to make their own decisions. He thought they should be told what to do. Trained like dumb animals.

Our American founders knew better. They knew that men and women could band together for their common good, as they did when they declared their independence from King George. But the founders also knew that maintaining such a free democracy would be a challenge. And so as Benjamin Franklin left the long convention that had finally drafted a Constitution, he announced what kind of government had been created, but added a warning, "A republic...if you can keep it."

Well, the verdict is still out. Today, the free-thinking men who founded and formed our great country have been replaced by the greedy zoo creatures that now run wild through our streets, across our TV screens, and down and into our hallowed halls of government. Darwin was not only wrong. It appears he had it exactly backwards.

And the risk of losing our republic continues to grow along with the swelling of our government, our taxes, our illegal immigrant population, and our cultural degeneracy. Still, it's not the people of America who should be enslaved and caged up. It's our leaders.

The American political system is a zoo. It's filled with an amazing array of animals: the squawking birds of the liberal aviary; the chatter-class monkeys, disdainful of the average American citizen; the microscopic political slime molds of the capital reflecting pools and the tidal basin; the deceptively cute denizens of the progressive petting zoo, hand-fed with tax-dollars; and the big game, including elected elephants and jackasses, all too comfortable in their collegial preserve and unaware of the lethal hold of the Potomac Pox that has infected them.

And as with the Disney empire, this Washington Zoo has set up its squawking franchises in other sites, most notably in Hollywood, where the birds of paradise sing and shriek from their gold-plated perches ("In that part of the world where Iran-mullah-supporting Sean Penn can pass for a pacifist, Kaballah-babbling Madonna can pass for a religious Jewish scholar of mysticism, and Rock Hudson could pass for a man's man"). And on the Hudson where the United Nations complex houses exotic imports including chameleons and vipers that deserve a particularly firm hand and watchful eye (especially the African Asp, Kofi Annan, who has "been at the center of more scandals than the Kennedys, the cast of *Diff'rent Strokes*, and the Minnesota Vikings combined").

And that's why this book is relevant, not just "funny." It's a guidebook to the world's political zoo, a reference for identifying the fierce beasts, pesky pests, dangerous reptiles, and menacing birds of prey that make up today's wild jungle of culture and politics. It will help you identify and label each of these unruly rulers.

As I lead you through the zoo, we will encounter a wide array of cold-blooded politicos and bird-brained pundits, every grunting, yelping, squawking breed of fish, fowl, or beast—from the porcupine called Bill O'Reilly ("a large terrestrial rodent well protected by its prickly exterior") to the mutated Long Island parrot Howard Stern (who was "bred accidentally on one of the Island's many toxic waste sites" and has "an uncanny ability to mimic the most vile comments that it hears and play them back with an added layer of verbal sewage").

We'll examine the eating habits of the amphibious Rush Limbaugh: "In a strange freak of nature, the Swell-Headed Bullfrog feeds primarily on its own ego."

We'll explore the natural habitat of the Kerry dolphin: "The Flipper family of Toothless Dolphins luxuriate in the protected coves of Cape Cod, Martha's Vineyard, and the South of France."

We'll take a look at the mating rituals of the Oily Armored Toad, Hugo Chavez: "Its mating habits are mostly unknown but most indications point to an excessive fetish for the almost-extinct island species, the *Cubanus dictatorum con beardus*."

We'll dissect the strange-yet-true gastric behaviors of the flatulent Hunchback Double-Striped Sloth, Larry King: "Does he wear those suspenders to keep his pants from falling down or to keep them from blowing off?"

We'll probe the dangers of the Ruth Gator Ginsburg ("This unseemly creature is easily the most aggressively progressive animal on the political zoo's Kangaroo Court and regularly tries to subvert the zoo's rules") and the Al Sharkton ("Maybe it's just me, but whenever I see him appear on the scene of some political event or racially-charged situation, I swear I can hear the *Jaws* theme playing in the background").

And we'll even get a glimpse at some circus sideshow attractions, from Cindy Shame-ham, the dancing bear who has been taught to dance the Bush Bash by her liberal handlers, to the high-flying, death-defying freak-turned-ringmaster Wolf Boy, Bill Clinton: "His was less of a presidency, really, than a French farce."

Yes, all of the most popular and infamous creatures of the political landscape—some good, some bad, some friendly, and some ferocious—are recognized and analyzed in this pertinent guidebook.

So join the Good Doctor, your resident biologist and trusty zookeeper, as we pass the cages of today's political beasts. But remember to obey the rules:

1. Do not try to pet the animals. Although many appear domesticated, almost all have a worse bite than week-old guacamole.

2. Do not feed the animals. They receive far too many handouts, and most of their bellies are already stuffed with government pork.

3. Do not leave your valuables unattended. Many of these scavengers are experts at taking your hard-earned money and using it to feather their own nests.

4. Be careful where you step. These animals have different standards of hygiene, to say the least, and take great pleasure in leaving their droppings everywhere. Like rabbits, they are not above eating it and might just expect the same of you.

Be aware.

And enjoy the tour.

Kofi Annan
Scandalon aspus

KoFi ANNaN

[*Scandalon aspus*]

Known popularly as the African Scandal Asp, this elusive creature moves effortlessly through international scandals and personal intrigues as quickly as water sinks into the Saharan sands. The Scandal Asp can be easily identified from other snakes, as it is the only species featuring pinstripe body markings instead of rings. Though native to Ghana, it finds the east side of Manhattan more hospitable, and a Swedish mate more attractive, than those found in its indigenous home. Potentially deadly when forced to action, and quite clever at subterfuge and camouflage, it will quickly disappear back into its diplomatic hole at the sight of any U.S. government auditor. When trapped, it will spray a hazy mist, scientifically called the "Force of International Law," to evade predators. The Scandal Asp maintains itself by consuming vast amounts of food and oil, providing adequate nutrition from which to suckle its young.

2

You just never know about Kofi Annan. You never know whether he's utterly inept or completely corrupt. Given that this is the United Nations we're talking about, I'd bet my money on both.

When United Nations employees recently evaluated his performance, they gave him a resounding vote of "no confidence." Now mind you, these are U.N. bureaucrats, most of whom are chin-deep in graft and corruption themselves. The competence bar here is lower than even at your local DMV (the Department of Mexican Votes).

So when this reptile house says it's time for Secretary Scandal to go, the world should take note. Right?

Not likely.

This snake has been at the center of more scandals than the Kennedys, the cast of *Diff'rent Strokes*, and the Minnesota Vikings combined. He's just one Lewinsky away from hitting the big leagues Clinton-style. Yet no one to the left of the John Birch Society will challenge the king cobra of the Uninvited Nations.

When his friend, the U.N. High Commissioner for Refugees, was cited by an investigative panel for sexually harassing a subordinate, the African Asp personally dismissed the charges. Why, you ask? Could it have been that the accuser was an American female? And as he learned in the Clinton era, she had to have been a liar, a stalker, and/or a Republican prop.

Apparently, the fairer sex is fair game in Kofi Land, the African Asp's U.N. jungle—scratch that, "rainforest" (there are no jungles any more). But I'm not about to call this swamp a wetlands. The U.N. is an old fashioned political swamp of the lowest order, a Tammany Hall with less conscience and billions more in walking around money. Just look at the food-for-sex scheme perpetrated by U.N. troops stationed in the Congo. In early 2005, accusations were made against U.N. peacekeepers who traded food to starving citizens for sexual favors. Kofi's soldiers raped Congolese girls as young as eleven years old. A senior U.N. official from France ran an Internet pedophile ring (Quelle surprise!). A U.N. colonel from South Africa (or was that "South Beach") was accused of molesting his teenage male translators.

Was this the Congo or Neverland Ranch?

George W. Bush eats his salad with the wrong fork, and they call for impeachment. Where's the crowing of Barbra Streisand when Kofi's incompetence leads to mass rape?

The sad truth is this snake in the grass still has supporters. His biggest cheerleader is the *Old York Times*. When *Times* reporter Judith Miller began a series of scalding articles on the oil-for-food scandal at the U.N., former *Times* U.N. bureau chief Barbara Crossette arranged a behind-the-scenes backstabbing party for her colleague. In her online messages, however, it slipped

Crossette's mind to mention the lavish "Special Lifetime Achievement Award" she received from the U.N. Correspondents Association and the $12,000 "Barbara Crossette Dinner" that the U.N. Foundation hosted in her honor at the Harvard Club in 2002.

It gets worse. Emeritus *Times*man Russell Baker was among those plunging his knife in his imprisoned colleague's back. Just as bad in Baker's eyes as Miller's WMD coverage, she had moved on to "a new beat: discrediting the United Nations." That's like discrediting Scott Peterson or Enron, Russ. It's just not that hard. Baker finds Miller's new target ironic "since it was the success of the U.N.'s peaceful approach to controlling WMDs in Iraq that underlined the wrongheadedness of the pro-invasion clique that supplied Miller with 'scoops.'"

Yes, that's Pulitzer Prize-winning Russell Baker, Walter Duranty's heir apparent. As Accuracy in Media has reported, other journalists, like Ian Williams, U.N. correspondent for *The (Communist) Nation*, and Linda Fasulo, who covers the U.N. beat for NBC News, MSNBC, and National Public Radio, and many other Western journalists the U.N. refuses to name, have taken hordes of U.N. cash for "special projects" while still reporting for their news organizations. And the *Times* cans Judith Miller?

At least Kofi knows, just like Al Capone, how to spread the graft around.

Oh, don't get me going about the oil-for-food scandal. If ever there was a program that was built for corruption, this was it. Only after the invasion of Iraq by American and British forces did the pervasive fraud and duplicity by the African Asp and every other U.N. official involved in the Oil-for-Food program become clear.

And who did this serpent blame for the scandal? The Americans and the British. Who else?

"They knew about it!" he hissed to his New York media lackeys. Well, of course they knew about it. So did I and anyone else who gave ten seconds of common sense consideration to the situation.

Vast amounts of unreported money. Virtually no oversight. The protection of diplomatic immunity. Who would ever hold them back? Jimmy Carter?

But we did see a bit of Kofi's softer side in the affair. According to some reports, which may or may not ever be verified, he let his own son in on the take. How sweet. I guess the family that preys together stays together.

But we have to remember the real world consequences to the African Asp's corruption and incompetence go beyond the billions in U.S. taxpayer dollars that get flushed down the U.N. bureaucratic toilet.

The real consequences of this snake's failed policies are seen in the countless bodies of the victims that he has been charged to protect throughout his U.N. career.

The Serbs killed by NATO bombs.

The mass graves of Srebrenica.

The killing fields of Rwanda.

The genocide in Darfur.

As Stalin once said so eloquently, one death is a tragedy, a million deaths is a statistic.

If Annan is the most famous African now living, the most famous African now dead is arguably Cleopatra. After the defeat of her lover, Marc Antony, and his subsequent suicide, she did not want to continue living in humiliation, even if comfortable. So she turned to the most reliable dispenser of poison she knew, the asp, and she let the asp do what it's best at.

The African Asp, as Kofi Annan gives proof, has no such shame. And far from eating its own tail, and sparing himself and the rest of the world the indignity of his tenure, this shady, poisonous snake continues to spinelessly slither through the political garden, never baring his teeth and striking when he's needed most. And just like the serpent of Eden, the Annan Asp (through corruption or incompetence—it makes no difference) contributes irrevocably to the fall of humanity.

Alec Baldwin
Notalentus anti-americanus

ALeC BALDWIN

The Santa Monica Stuffed Turkey is a corpulent bird with an increasingly thick wattle. This unlovely fowl promises to fly the coop after every election until remembering that it can't fly at all. The bird has been spotted in the wild, but only in old movies. In reality, this indulged gobbler could not endure for a long weekend among its free ranging kin. Although a member of the chicken family, it occasionally threatens to kill and dismember certain elected officials and their families. It is also known to attack the annoying Italian pest known as paparazzi, all the while feigning pacifism. The Santa Monica Stuffed Turkey is the largest, roundest, and most malodorous of its family and genus and an easy target for hunters eager to thin the turkey population.

9

Alec Baldwin is one of the most versatile actors in Hollywood.
His acting just doesn't translate very well to the screen.
Indeed, in movies he shows all the versatility of a toaster.
Once outside of his plush Santa Monica habitat, however,
he really starts acting. Acting up, that is. Or acting out.
And, in the process, exorcising the demons that haunt him.

We all remember when on national TV—in a manic
tirade that prefigured Howard Dean—he threatened to
stone Congressman Henry Hyde and his family to *death*.
Hyde's sin was to help impeach a lying, obstructing president. Baldwin's response was to threaten to lead a Malibu
mob with pitchforks and torches to defend the honor of
Bill Clinton. Those were the days.

Of late, Baldwin has been only slightly more successful
in resuscitating his career than Gary Coleman has with
his. The Stuffed Turkey plays the occasional cameo in
movies requiring a fat guy and appears every now and
then on *Will and Grace*, TV's weekly gay pride parade.
Mostly, however, he shows up in Left Coast courtrooms to
do battle with his lovely ex-wife, Kim Basinger, who had
the good sense to shake and bake.

Recent photos indicate that this turkey is inclined to
pre-stuff itself with every kind of fattener from tube steak
to starch out of the box. In other words, "Hide the
Cheetos, Martha. Here comes Bigfoot!" Yet notice that he
still tries to cram his eighteen-inch neck into a fifteen-
inch shirt. The rest of the wattle spills over his collar in

the style of his mentor, the gelatinous Senator Edward Kennedy.

Yet, in a classic bit of Malibu logic, the one thing this not-so-smart Alec *won't* eat is goose pate. Why? Because our rock-throwing stoner claims the geese who provide this snobbish delicacy are mistreated.

The Stuffed Turkey felt so strongly about this injustice that he publicly cried "fowl" and now spends his otherwise idle days fighting for goose rights. (No, I'm not kidding). He even reached out to the dying Pope John Paul II! "Your words would do a world of good for God's animals," he pontificated to the astonished pontiff.

Maybe Baldwin confuses real life with a plot from one of his cheesy, made-for-cable movies. I can see the scene now. Pope Santa Monica I—more jowls and hair perhaps than people expect in a pope, but jolly nonetheless—meets with his trusted Cardinal confidante skillfully played by Alan Alda. "Your Holiness, where would you like to start today?" says the Cardinal. "AIDS in Botswana? Famine in Bangladesh? Pedophilia in Boston?"

"No," says the pontiff with great solemnity, rubbing his ample stubble, "First things first. I need to deal with this horrific goose pate situation!" Next thing you know, Baldwin will be urging his equally daft crony, Richard Gere, to have the Dalai Lama intercede.

It gets worse. The same Malibu logic that rebels against goose-whacking is A-OK with partial birth abortion. Indeed, this turkey has no problem with crushing the skull of a near full-term fetus and sucking out the brain, provided, of course, it is not the skull of a goose. He'll tell you as much himself, and expect you to understand. His fans do.

Of course, this kind of wisdom is not unique to the Stuffed Turkey. It infects his whole side of the aisle. His fowl-minded philosophy has elevated Baldwin to a position of authority within the Democratic Party. In fact, at the 2004 Democratic National Convention, the powers that be put Baldwin on a panel to discuss the Supreme Court. What, was senior judicial analyst Brad Pitt unavailable?

But before you start scratching your head and asking what kind of expertise a Baldwin brother could possibly have about our highest judiciary, let me remind you of his credentials. He played the assistant district attorney in *Ghosts of Mississippi*. His film company produced a cable movie on the Nuremburg trials. By Democrat standards, that would move him up to scholar status. Heck, maybe he should have replaced Rehnquist.

Still, what most people remember of Alec, the political blowhard, is his claim that he would leave the country should George W. win the 2000 election.

Bon voyage, moron.

Now Baldwin denies he ever made the claim.

Sorry, Alec. Such stale acting may have cut it in *Pearl Harbor* but not while Savage holds the keys to the cages. Alec Bald-faced-lie had his original statement caught on tape and verified by people within earshot. People like his own wife.

Oh, if only he *had* flown south for the winter. We could have finally been rid of one of the shrillest birds in the Hollywood cage. And Alec might have made some Guatemalan theater troupe very happy.

"Harry Belafonte"
Gone bananas

HARRY BeLa FoNTe

The Large-Mouthed Faux-Jamaican Loon is a small-brained creature whose native habitat is New York City, where it was hatched, but which has established a bogus identity as being from Jamaica, a region in which it spent a few years of its early birdhood. With a diet consisting primarily of nuts and fruitcake, its enormous oral orifice allows it to swallow large quantities of Venezuelan and Cuban gruel and regurgitate it at will. The Large-Mouthed Loon is one of the few birds that contracts a bizarre form of dementia, and can do so at an early age.

You could blame old age for much of the madness of Harry Belafonte, but the sad truth is that he's demonstrated serious mental decline for decades. Yet instead of putting him on a road tour with the Penguins and Bobettes and other one-hit wonders of the fifties, the Left seems insistent on trotting out Crazy Uncle Harry to be some sort of philosophical spokesmodel.

Thank God for fellow traveler Cindy Shame-ham or Belafonte would be the flat out looniest loon in the neo-Bolshevik Jungle. And at least she's got an excuse— although I can hear Katie Couric claiming the Large-Mouthed Loon to be above criticism too. After all, Katie might say, "America has denied this proud bird a hit record for the last fifty years just because it is a loon. This is worse than bigotry. This is loon-acy." I don't exaggerate about the fifty years. His one big hit album—*Calypso*—debuted in 1956. Not too long after that, he was thrilled to get a gig on *The Muppet Show*.

There's not much that escapes the loon's steel-trap maw, but while touring Kenya in 2004 as UNICEF's "goodwill" ambassador, Belafonte expressed his shock at the level of poverty in Africa. Really? Shocked at the poverty in Africa? Who would have ever guessed? That discovery led him into a rant about how some Kenyans lived very well, while most others lived in squalor. Just like in Los Angeles. And it was all Bush's fault anyhow.

No one can deny the Large-Mouthed Loon's impeccable credentials as a useful idiot, and there is no longer even a "savant" part to compensate. The man who once praised Ho Chi Minh as a great leader was most recently seen and heard denouncing the Department of Homeland Security as the Gestapo. He made his comments while standing beside Hugo Chavez, who is busy turning Venezuela into a first rate Banana Republic, the kind of place with which this loon can identify. "Hey, Mr. Taliban, Tally me bananas!"

In Chavez World, Belafonte shared the stage with Hugo, Danny Glover, and Cornel West—the Moe, Larry, and Curly of radical politics—which grouping gave ample testament to the fact that birds of a certain pinkish feather do flock together.

Since no one wanted him to sing "The Banana Boat Song"—no please, Harry, not again—Belafonte did a little karaoke number called the "World's Greatest Terrorist." He sang not of Hugo Chavez, but—surprise, surprise—of President Bush.

So over the top were the Large-Mouthed Loon's comments that the AARP—The American Association of Ridiculous People—which he had joined about forty years ago, denounced him. A short time earlier, the AARP had named him one of its ten "Impact Award" nominees. Yes, the Large-Mouthed Loon has impact all right, similar in kind if not size to the impact a terrorist plane has on a crowded World Trade Center.

How could the AARP possibly profess shock? This loon has been behaving badly in public for decades. There's hardly a totalitarian leader in the past thirty years that hasn't called Belafonte "comrade." In 1983, the Banana Boat Bozo was speaking at an event organized by the East German government (Boy, did those guys know how to karaoke! Day-O!) denouncing America's installation of Pershing missiles in West Germany. Do you think he complained about the SS-20 nuclear missiles that the Soviets were installing all over Eastern Europe, including East Germany? Well, no, that would have required either some shred of common sense or at least a teeny bit of affection for the country that nurtured him. The Large-Mouthed Loon is notorious for biting the hand that feeds it.

Just a few years before his AARP Award, this bigoted bird called Colin Powell and Condi Rice "house niggers," the kind that "lived in the house with the master." Said Condi in response, "I don't need Harry Belafonte to tell me what it means to be black." She didn't get the AARP award. He did.

And then there's the loon's love affair with Fidel Castro. What's not to love? The Large-Mouthed Loon was so enamored with the Cuban dictator that he starred in Hollywood's 2002 biopic on the man. In 2000, he partied with Castro to commemorate the memory of convicted and executed Communist spies, Julius and Ethel Rosenberg, both guilty of stealing our atomic secrets. In 2003, this loon was one of Hollywood's more useful idiots to sign a petition in support of Castro's absurdly oppressive regime.

As documented in Humberto Fontova's book, *Fidel: Hollywood's Favorite Tyrant*, Belafonte bristled when challenged about his Castro bootlicking: "If you believe in freedom! If you believe in justice, if you believe in democracy—you have no choice but to support Fidel Castro!" I'm sure the thousands rotting in Fidel's political prisons would love to school this birdbrain in Castro's Bizarro World version of life, liberty, and the pursuit of happiness.

The Large-Mouthed Loon, of course, was willing to overlook the scores of thousands murdered and the hundreds of thousands forced to flee at the risk of their lives. Why not? Wasn't their literacy rate the highest in Latin America?

The only problem was that Cuba, among its other eccentricities, inherited a Soviet-style squeamishness about homosexuality. For Castro, like Stalin, homosexuality was a "bourgeois decadence" and "capitalist degeneration." He declared homosexuality illegal, punishable by four years imprisonment, and forced parents to rat out their children and neighbors or risk their own freedom. This led to midnight raids on gays and forced dispatch to prison camps for "reeducation" and "rehabilitation." Some homosexuals simply "disappeared." At the time, the

Large-Mouthed Loon did not yet know that he was supposed to be outraged by homophobia, not homosexuality—so he didn't make a chirp of protest.

In 1992, aware that he might be making the queens of Hollywood uncomfortable, Castro told an interviewer, "I am absolutely opposed to any form of repression, contempt, scorn, or discrimination with regard to homosexuals," and everything was not just forgiven but forgotten. On the Left, all you have to do is say you're for or against something. You don't have to do jack. In Castro's island prison, gays with AIDS are quarantined on a separate island!

Daylight come and me wants this loon to go home. If that home is Jamaica, Venezuela, or Cuba, all the better, just as long as it's not New York where he was born. The Large-Mouthed Loon has been faking his Third-World identity for the bulk of his nicely feathered existence. Let's see how he adapts to those lovely Third-World "rain forests" without the protection of his U.S. passport.

BoNo

[Gaelic shamus]

The tiny well-fed Irish Chicken, or Bono, can most often be spotted in front of any available bank of cameras, squawking for American taxpayer funding of its various pet causes, even though this particular species offers none of his own scratch. It is generally suspected that the Irish Chicken suffers from a congenital eye condition, making it oversensitive to light (or, as some scientists suggest, willfully blind), hence its ever-present wraparound shades. Despite this fowl's piercing, grating voice, the Bono is known to attract political fowl of diverse speciation and is frequently confused as an animal of some importance. It also lays many eggs, often rotten (e.g., Zooropa).

For reasons I still can't fathom, Paul David Hewson, the fowl known as "Bono," is allowed to run wild wherever he pleases, a free-range chicken in the weirdest sense of the word. But because he thrives on the limelight, there is one sure way to capture this wandering scavenger: Put a lens in front of him. Whether he's prancing and clucking about the stage at one of his band's lyrically-challenged and overwrought concerts or mugging into a news camera, this brogued begging bird can only consistently squawk one word: "Gimme."

The lead singer of the Irish rock band U2 has abused his pop star popularity to promote pie-in-the-sky leftwing causes for years. The Guinness-bred Gael once was a vocal advocate for Greenpeace—right up until their little run-in with the French government resulted in their boat being blown out of the water. It was soon thereafter that instead of saving whales, Bozo the Baffling decided to channel his efforts at something more attainable and less lofty . . . eliminating Third-World poverty and AIDS.

What's next, almighty Bono? A worldwide stand against sadness. An end to B.O.? A cure for death?

Yet amazingly, in spite of all his head-in-the-clouds, face-in-the-sand posturing, Bono is still universally fawned over. This tiresome tenor was even nominated for a Nobel Prize! Perhaps the committee confused him with Sonny Bono, a duly elected member of the House of Representatives who really did deserve a Peace Prize for maintaining tranquility between himself and his body-tucked ex, the ubiquitous female impersonator known as Cher.

Or perhaps it's because Bono was awarded the Legion of Honor from Jacques Chirac. A citizenship award from a French president? Isn't that like receiving the Husband of the Year Award from Robert Blake?

I can understand the liberal lackeys at CBS's *60 Minutes* promoting the agenda of this Dublin dilettante, but members of our own government? I mean, don't get me wrong. I've always hoped that Senate Majority Leader Bill Frist would give Senator Diane "Ho Chi" Feinstein a good working over, but to see him practically tackle her to get to the head of the photo-op line for a picture with Bono? What gives?

But apparently meeting with our congressional leaders wasn't good enough for this troubadour of tripe. He was actually able to finagle a face-to-face with our president.

Imagine, with our crucial war against terrorism going full-throttle, our commander-in-chief took time from his duties to meet with this charlatan in his wraparound shades. I guess White House handlers thought a meeting between the beleaguered Bush and the beloved Bono would help boost the president's ratings, even if none of his fans has ever been sober enough on an election day to vote.

So exactly what does the Irish Chicken want from us?

What any chicken wants: scratch. He wants our money. And he wants lots of it.

Now understand that this prosperous (and preposterous) bird has a personal net worth that's more than the budget of every Third-World country he claims to represent. But the only money that works for him is from the hardworking, American, middle-class taxpayer. He'll take Canadian money, too. Last year, Bono berated the even more pathologically self-loathing Canadian Prime Minister Paul Martin for not giving enough, and the bash, broadcast on the CBC, helped assure Martin's narrow defeat in 2006 at the hands of the stingier conservative party. Make my day, ay! Maybe there is "social justice" in this world after all.

But wait. Isn't Pro Bono a taxpayer, too? Hold on to your W2s, ladies and gentlemen, because this is where the luck of the Irish flourishes. Bono recently told a British tabloid, "You know, we pay a lot of tax by the way, a lot of tax, enormous, millions of tax." However, the truth is that under an Irish law designed to keep artists and entertainers from fleeing the Old Sod for the New World, Bono pays no personal income taxes whatsoever on his enormous music royalties. And there is no property tax in Ireland either. And, through a series of shell corporations in Ireland and abroad—some of which carry heavy losses—Bono and his band mates pay virtually no tax at all. So there you have it: rock-star socialism in all its hysterical and hypocritical glory.

Don't get me wrong. I'm all for doing whatever we can to combat the brutality of this world. But we're not going to sing it in to extinction. All the serenading politicians, politicos, and media groupies with songs of a world free of famine, poverty, disease, and warfare will in the end only help the serenading politicians, politicos, and media groupies. The poor will suffer just as before, and their musical tastes will suffer even more. Wake up, Bonehead. This is life, not a 1970s Coca-Cola commercial.

If you really want to end worldwide suffering, stop playing *With or Without You.*

So, you ask, if Bono's approach to alleviating world hunger is nothing more than a leprechaun's crock at the end of the rainbow, what's my solution?

Simple. First, we put all our resources into wiping terrorism—and all the bomb-toting jihadists that go with it—off the face of the earth. Once that mission is accomplished, we can ban foreigners from playing rock and roll. Then, we can get back to reestablishing our country as the strongest, hardest-working, most generous society ever—a society that has historically reached out to less fortunate countries.

But instead of *forgiving*, as Bozo would have us do with the debts owed us, we would once again become a society of giving. Giving and sharing our technologies—agricultural and otherwise—to help needy countries help themselves out of poverty. Also, we might just share the gifts of free enterprise, the rule of law, and private property rights. Bono's into fishes. Savage is into fishing poles.

So that's the Savage Solution. Take it for what it's worth. But don't be duped into thinking that a forty-six-year-old Peter Pan wannabe who parades around a stage in leather pants begging fifteen-year-old girls to come up and dance with him is the answer.

Don't let this shaded chicken rule the roost.

And if my advice isn't good enough for you, heed the words of one of the more intelligent members of the rock-and-roll species, Alice Cooper, who recently told journalists, "If you're listening to rock stars in order to get your information on who to vote for, you're a bigger moron than they are."

Rock on.

Barbara Boxer
Californiae cacklus

BaRBaRa BoXeR

[*Californiae cacklus*]

The California Cackle Hen is indigenous to Brooklyn, New York, but regularly migrates to the Left Coast after maturation, where it can better peck itself up the food chain. Known for its erratic and eccentric behaviors, the Cackle Hen has the ability to foul the air as a defense mechanism to compensate for its lack of reason and basic instinct. The smallest bird in the Savage Zoo, the Cackle Hen compensates with a tough demeanor and a willingness to provoke confrontations with its natural enemies. Although this might seem to indicate a propensity for physical aggression, when cornered to fight, the inherent nature of the poultry family prevails and prompts the Cackle Hen to retreat to its coop. Indeed, its first novel—a rare feat for a chicken—is tellingly titled *A Time to Run.*

If there is any example in American politics that anyone—absolutely anyone—can go from asking people "Would you like a size 38D?" to the highest echelons of the American political zoo, it is Barbara Boxer. Although a Levy at birth, the Cackle Hen, as the shortest member of the Senate, brings a box with her to any podium where she has to speak (thus the name "Boxer").

The heartthrob of the extremist-Left, the Cackle Hen mans the farthest outposts of unreality in the Democratic Party, along with fellow-traveler Rep. Cynthia McKinney and the rest of the "Hate America First" congressional caucus.

A party loyalist, in 1994 the Cackle Hen sacrificed her only daughter, Nicole, to the lamentable Rodham family in a White House ceremony. The presidency outlasted the marriage, as Nicole impeached Tony Rodham a few years after the sacrifice.

That President Clinton survived his own impeachment is a testament to the mind-boggling duplicity of the Cackle caucus in the U.S. Senate. While still in the House, the Cackle Hen proudly authored the original Violence Against Women Act and co-sponsored it in the Senate. The bill empowered Paula Jones to pursue her suit against the president. Boxer called the president's behavior in the Jones and Lewinsky matter "indefensible" but then promptly fell on her sword defending him and it. Said *The Wall Street Journal* with some understatement: "The feminists have impaled themselves with their Clinton defense. Who can possibly take their next moral crusade seriously? Barbara Boxer has earned cult status in the annals of political hypocrisy."

This Madame Defarge of Marin County serves as a road bump in the path of American progress and international justice. And the chief victims of her obstruction seem inevitably to be women, especially conservative black women and the unborn.

Can anyone forget the confrontation between the Cackle Hen and Condoleezza Rice at her nomination hearings for secretary of state? Boxer strutted into this hen party/cockfight unarmed. Has there ever been a more mismatched battle of wits? Here sits Rice—current national security advisor, former provost of Stanford University, world-renowned scholar of Soviet and Russian politics, Olympic swimmer, classically-trained concert pianist—being heckled by a yenta, who back in Sheepshead Bay would have been content to mismanage a small lingerie shop. We're talking about a woman who proclaimed to the world in a May 2002 Senate Commerce Committee meeting that communism in Cuba was "dead." No, Barb, it is freedom and justice and scores of thousands of freedom lovers that are dead.

Of course, no one has ever associated great political skill or intellectual acuity with the Cackle Hen. She has ended up on the wrong side of virtually every major political question since her election to the Senate. *And whatever it is she says*, to paraphrase Marx (Groucho, not Karl), *I'm against it*—privatizing Social Security, ANWR, and, of course, the War in Iraq ("the best vote of my life" as she bragged to fellow Munchkin, Jon Stewart). She is somewhat less proud of her vote *for* No Child Left Behind.

As one of the most vocal critics of the Iraq War, the Cackle Hen complains that we should have waited for an international consensus before taking military action. Yea, maybe at some point France and Russia would have wearied of soaking billions out of Iraq in the Food-for-Oil scam and agreed to kill the goose that laid the golden egg. Right.

And what was Madame Defarge's position on the first Gulf War when there was a vast international coalition aligned with the U.S. to evict her pen pal Saddam from Kuwait? As a member of the House of Representatives, she voted against the use of force.

Maybe she felt that international consensus was overrated.

Maybe she was afraid Saddam would stop writing.

So why do the California fools of the Left Coast keep reelecting her—and by ever increasing margins at that? Maybe it's her overwhelming compassion in the midst of tragedy. Take for instance her comments to a reporter after one of California's most damaging natural disasters.

"Those who survived the San Francisco earthquake said, 'Thank God I'm still alive,'" Boxer commented. "But, of course, those who died—their lives will never be the same again."

Or is it really her war chest from the abortion racket and her ties to Indian gambling interests, as many say who have studied this bird's rise to power?

The textbook example is how she pushed for federal recognition of a small group of landless Indians, the Coast Miwok, that had promised not to use their new status to promote gambling in Marin or Sonoma Counties. That promise lasted four months (longer than any campaign promise from Democrats), before the Indian tribe was negotiating with a Las Vegas casino company to build a monumental casino, much to the consternation of the locals.

Enter the Cackle Hen's own son, Dougie Boxer, whose well-connected Democratic law firm was hired to lobby for the Indian tribe and also to broker the land deal for the new casino. Yes, the Cackle Hen is very protective of her chicks, even involving them in her chicken scratch schemes.

But the casino project threatened vast environmental damage to the surrounding natural habitat. Surely Earth Mother Barbara Boxer wouldn't stand for that, would she? Well, she will when there's serious chicken feed at stake.

Because she pushed for federal recognition, the Indian tribe was no longer required to abide by local and state environmental regulations. Remember that old TV commercial with the Indian crying over pollution? Now he's crying because his tribe didn't have Barbara Boxer's help to build their casino first.

And the dirty dealings seem to spread through the Boxer household like chicken pox. Consider Barbara's husband, Stewart, the rooster of the pen, who makes his living suing companies for worker's compensation claims. On the same day in 2003, he wrote two $1,750 checks, one under the name Stewart and another under the name Stuart. According to election cycle 2004 FEC records, Stewart listed his employer as Boxer & Gerson; Stuart said he was employed by Noxer & Gerson. One gave to Boxer's 2004 Senate campaign; the other to the Boxer/DSCC '04 Committee, Barbara's authorized PAC.

The problem is, of course, that this was a blatant go-around of federal law, which at the time limited individual campaign contributions to $2,000 per candidate. But wasn't Barbara Boxer a vocal supporter of the Bipartisan Campaign Reform Act of 2002, which would have banned these soft-money go-arounds?

Yes, the Cackle Hen has learned all the tricks in the Washington coop, which brings us to her barely literate literature, *A Time to Run*. Only the bravest political pundits inside the Beltway have dared to venture into the maddeningly boring plot of this novel. None have returned to make sense of it.

A generally positive review on Amazon gives you some sense of the book's character: "I have to admit that I found some of these [sex scenes] to be amusing. The horse sex scene was an obvious metaphor for rape and for the oppression and objectification of women. The 'knee cap' reference I didn't quite get. The others, I did. Imagine that distinguished senator knowing about sex!" Although this reviewer called the book a "fun read," he added, "How about a little more subtlety next time! This isn't campaign literature!"

And yet now there's a grassroots campaign to draft the Cackle Hen—equestrian intercourse and all—to run for president in 2008. Remember this hen going out of her way to criticize Tom Delay for hiring members of his family for his campaign committees and PACs? She just forgot to mention she paid her son, Doug Boxer, $130,000 to do the same. See what I mean? The Cackle Hen has real presidential potential, if the Democratic Party record is any standard of measure.

Boxer must also walk delicately around the Jack Abramoff scandal. As it happens, her favorite governor, Gray Davis, accepted two million dollars from gambling interests in his various campaigns and then presided over the largest expansion of gambling in U.S. history, legalizing just about every kind of dollar-sucking device the gambling industry has yet to invent.

As for your friendly zookeeper, at the end of the day, I lose no sleep. I have seen enough of this peculiar breed of chicken to feel confident that the American people will not let her turn the White House into a Hen House, at least not in my lifetime.

George W. Bush

Stingus bumblus

GeoRGe W. BUSH

[*Stingus bumblus*]

The Texas Bumblebee was transplanted from the East Coast where it evolved into a hardier, more persistent species. Its natural enemies, like the donkey, are constantly underestimating the bee's sting. They think that a good swat or two should dispatch this gritty little bumblebee to oblivion, and even after repeated stings, they refuse to learn their lesson. The same holds true for many foreign species, like the Iraqi desert rats and the Afghan weasels, both now nearly extinct after challenging the seemingly innocuous bumblebee in its very own habitat. The Texas Bumblebee insists on pollinating the world with Texas-style notions of freedom and fair play, whether the world is ready for them or not.

38

George W. Bush does sometimes put the "bumble" in bumblebee. And some of the deals he's pushed, like turning over our ports to a state-sponsored Arab company, are the kind of blunders that cause this bee to sting himself in the tail.

The Texas Bumblebee scared me the moment I heard him run under the banner of "compassionate conservative," a term I coined but never imagined would be cashed in so often. Governments can't be compassionate, Tex. Only people can. To be compassionate, it's got to be your own money on the table. I was afraid we were in for another four years of raising taxes and throwing up on Japanese prime ministers, and then those Islamofascist termites bored their way into our world and brought it crashing down around us.

It was only then that I realized the difference between a Texas Bumblebee and a Connecticut one. Given its environment, the Texas Bumblebee's got grit. It's got sand. OK, Bush may have spent much of his youth pickled up to his wing pits, but that pickling may well have preserved his will. Something did.

And we all know Washington needs it.

After September 11, the Texas Bumblebee told those sand ants in the Middle East that our soldier ants were coming to pull some wings. The sand ants snickered. They shouldn't have. The Texas Bumblebee buzzed right on in, leaving the desert littered with sand fleas.

The two most odious pests in that part of the world soon found themselves hiding in holes. The only difference between Saddam and Osama is that we've turned over Saddam's rock. Although Osama has been about as useful to his cause as his cave's stalagmites. Meanwhile, the Orkin men found their way to Uday and Qusay.

Back in America, the jackasses rallied behind the Texas Bumblebee until about the first commercial break on September 11, and then they started showing their true colors, all of them shades of yellow. When the Iraq War didn't end in ninety-six hours like the last one, they started braying that they had been betrayed. Don't all wars end in four days?

Meanwhile, Howling Howie Dean, the one jackass candidate who did not get a chance to waffle on Iraq (being that no one was listening), started making a virtue of his premature treason. Once he tapped into the world of lefty blogheads, all of his opponents started to imitate him. It didn't matter to them that in the age of the Internet, every dire warning they had made about WMDs could be called up at the touch of the "Return" button. It didn't matter how they had voted on Iraq, they just couldn't let Howling Howie flank them on the Cindy Shame-ham left.

And so we had a mad rush for the Benedict Arnold Humanitarian award by just about every Dem to the south of Joe Lieberman, which is all of them, especially Jimmy Carter, who with Yasser Arafat took the Swedish version of the prize.

Now, just about every Dem fool enough to leave his Kerry-Edwards sticker on his bumper rushes to the TV each morning hoping the American body count has gone up in Iraq. Yes, "hoping." Admit it, you jackasses! Not knowing history, it eludes them that in the Vietnam War the daily body count was more than seven times as high as in Iraq, in Korea more than fifteen times as high, and in World War II, more than a hundred times as high in a country then only half as populated. The libs would have been demanding we pull out of France because we didn't take Berlin in four days.

You want a little history. In World War I, the British took sixty thousand casualties on the first day of the Battle of the Somme. In the following few months, they lost one million men. With 1/6 of our population base, the Brits didn't whine half as much. What makes Cindy Shame-ham so special is that the young soldiers who are getting killed are not the children of the Left. The Left stopped having children about forty years ago. Those few that survived their parents' drug use and contraceptives—or worse—are pierced voluntarily and scarred only by their tattoos.

Leftists, young and old, don't even know what side

they are on. Canada could invade us today, and they would want to surrender. It's that bad. The Texas Bumblebee deserves better.

Not knowing history and refusing to know anything about the present beyond one's blog of choice, a recycled herd of lefty lemmings has focused its mindless wrath on the bumblebee, who is trying his best to save their whiny little selves. This is how the "Hate the Bumblebee" pandemic spread throughout blue state America. The candidates had no other agenda to campaign on but their comparative hatred of Tex. Never has so innocuous a bumblebee generated so much sheer rage. I just keep wishing he'd given them something big to hate him for. But the Texas Bumblebee continues to disappoint me by being so nice, even to such reptilian creeps like the Clintons and Teddy Kennedy. C'mon, Texas, we need a little more Old Testament in the mix, a little more righteous wrath.

But Tex ignores them and keeps bumbling on. He has just succeeded in getting Sam Alito nominated to the Supreme Court, not bad for a guy who was finished, or at least so *Time* magazine told us. If you know me, I've had my issues with Tex—and God only knows what he was thinking about with the "Ozzie and Harriet" Miers nomination—but his two successful Supreme Court picks alone justify your not voting for the Munster brothers, Al and John.

The fact that the Alito vote was relatively close—58 to 42—inspired the wonderfully absurd spectacle of the two Massachusetts senators trying to psych their fellow jackasses into a filibuster, but much too close to happy hour to succeed. By the way, Ted, it's "Alito" not "Alioto." Alioto was the mayor out here back when Democrats could still be patriots and human beings.

With a few years left in his presidency, it's too early to say how history will judge Tex. My guess is that we will come to think of him much as we do Harry Truman, a relatively simple, straightforward mid-American, not sophisticated enough to have mastered the art of kowtowing. Like Truman, Tex was handed a heavy load, and like Truman, he has not shirked.

Unlike Truman, however, Tex went to Congress for authorization of his military ventures in a part of the world that was hugely more critical than Korea, and where our chances of success are higher and our casualties dramatically lower. Besides, as bad as some of Tex's domestic stuff is, it's not half as bad as Harry's—public housing, anyone?—and he has never thought to call it a "Fair Deal."

But he is giving the jackasses a run for their money in the government spending department. In his two terms, Bill Clinton increased discretionary spending by 10 percent; in just his first term, Tex increased it by 25 percent.

Overall, the federal budget under Bush has been increasing twice as fast as under Clinton—an increase any New Deal jackass would love. The last time that federal spending grew so fast was under Nixon/Ford, not nearly the Republican team he should be trying to emulate.

Now he's tried to buzz around that fact by promising in his recent State of the Union address to throw around enough tax money to make everybody happy. Then there are the tens of billions of tax dollars thrown around after Hurricane Katrina like cheap plastic necklaces during Mardi Gras. But somebody is going to have to pay for all this, as they're finding out in Texas after Bush's tenure running that state's hive. Unless federal spending is cut at some point, we are either going to have rapid inflation or tax increases. That's economics simple enough even for a bumbling bee.

And then we have Social Security and our national borders to deal with, and there's no one better than a second term president to do the right thing. But the bee has failed us miserably on the borders. Where Clinton opened the border with Mexico, Bush has taken the door off the hinges. The porkers in Congress don't have the courage to lift their snouts out of the trough for fear of stirring up the hornet's nest back at home in their congressional district.

But Tex's greatest blessing politically is that his opponents, and even his supporters, have always underestimated him. He was supposedly so stupid, Al would crush him in the debate. He didn't. OK, then, John would. He didn't. Surely, they would beat him in the elections. They haven't. Tex has stung the jackasses four times in a row— a perfect record—including Governor Ann Richards who was sure she'd swat him down. She didn't.

Liberals continue to think of politics as a picnic, where they can eat, drink, and be nasty at Tex's expense. It's only when they get stung again and again that they remember that this bumblebee still hasn't lost his sting.

Robert Byrd
kracker kornbred krookus

RoBeRT BYRD

[Kracker kornbred krookus]

Although almost universally mistaken for fowl, because of its name and the way it mysteriously glides above much-deserved criticism, the Robert Byrd is really an example of the rare West Virginia White-Hooded Rat (or Ratbyrd), a rodent with an unusually long life cycle. With an insatiable appetite for pork, which it eats directly from the barrel, the White-Hooded Rat will often engorge itself to the point of embarrassment. This rodent has also been known to form predatory packs with other White Hoods and to attack anything or anyone that is not a White-Hooded Rat. This species has been so historically prominent in West Virginia that every other street, school, and sewer in the state is named after it.

A man of many monikers, Senator Robert Byrd, the White-Hooded Rat, has been called "the conscience of the Senate," "the soul of the Democratic Party," and the "love of my life" (by Senator Barbara Boxer—sorry Stu). Some of his less-flattering, although equally well-known, sobriquets include "The King of Congressional Pork," "Boss Hogg," "Sheets Byrd," and last, but certainly not least, the "Klan Kleagle."

That's right. The senator from West Virginia, venerated by his fellow Democrats, was an active member of the Ku Klux Klan when he was in his twenties. Not only did he belong, he also actually *recruited* over 150 men to form a local chapter, eventually rising to the level of "Grand Kleagle." And the Byrd droppings just keep on coming, yes indeed. Because of his oversized efforts, he was chosen the "Exalted Cyclops," which is the top elected officer in any local Klan unit. Imagine that! The Democratic Party's poster child for conscience spent more time under a hood than Mr. Goodwrench!

And yet there are those who believe this White-Hooded Rat when he chalks it all off to "youthful indiscretion." That's what Hans Frank and Julius Streicher said at Nuremberg, but we weren't buying it there either, Ratbyrd. No, "youthful indiscretion" is yellowing your neighbor's snowman, mooning your high school principal, sneaking your college girlfriend into your parents' bedroom during spring break. But being an active participant—a recruiter, no less—for such a Neanderthal organization, during World War II even. That's no "youthful indiscretion." That's who you are. And the Senate Democrats fretted over the fact that Justice Alito belonged to the Concerned Alumni of Princeton! Should we laugh or cry?

And though Ratbyrd claims that his involvement in the KKK lasted only a few short months, the record indicates otherwise. Two years after he claimed to have changed his sheets, Byrd composed a letter to Senator Theodore Bilbo of Mississippi (real name, true story), in which he expressed his sentiments on integrating the military, never to fight "with a Negro by my side. Rather I should die a thousand times and see Old Glory trampled in the dirt, never to rise again, than to see this beloved land of ours become degraded by race mongrels, a throwback to the blackest specimen from the wilds." OK, and MSNBC fired Savage for what?

As it turned out, the White-Hooded Rat never had to worry about serving with any "race mongrels" by his side. To do that, he would have had to serve, and that's something this able-bodied senator-to-be did not get around to doing. It would have interfered with his wartime recruiting. A Kleagle's day is never done! For the record, the White-Hooded Rat did man the front lines in Baltimore with a welding torch.

Decades later, Ratbyrd joined with Senators William Fulbright, Al Gore Sr., and other liberal icons to derail every piece of civil rights legislation coming down the line. In that same period, the "conscience of the Senate" called Martin Luther King Jr. "a coward who got other people into trouble." When the semi-reconstructed Byrd voted against the nomination of Clarence Thomas to the Supreme Court, he earned the unique distinction of being the only senator to vote against both black nominees, Thurgood Marshall being the first.

And just a few years ago, the "soul of the Democratic party" told Fox News: "There are white niggers. I've seen a lot of white niggers in my time. I'm going to use that word."

This isn't a toothless, banjo-pickin' cousin-breeder right out of *Deliverance*, mind you. This is an eight-time elected U.S. senator—one "loved" by Barbara Boxer, the "conscience" of Flatbush.

Who is this hillbilly kidding? The only thing in the Senate more in the red than the budget is Senator Byrd's neck. And the only wise counsel this octagenarian can provide is how to get stubborn grass stains off white sheets.

You have to know the state of the intra-party competition to understand how this man has become the Democrats' master strategist and constitutional historian. For the big government party—hard to distinguish them nowadays—it's not about principle. It's about power. And after nearly half a century in the Senate, the White-

Hooded Rat has mastered the rodent-like art of getting it and hoarding it.

Over the years, as his political clout grew, Ratbyrd morphed from a hood-wearer into a hoodwinker, from a run-of-the-mill rodent to King Rat. In his role as chairman of the Senate Appropriations Committee, he has had almost unlimited access to the national granary, and he has been eating away at it ever since.

In his home state of West Virginia, more than thirty tax supported locations or institutions bear his name. Truth be told, he's got that name on more pork than Oscar Mayer. I won't get into the expected ego-massaging tributes: schools, streets, hospitals, etc. I'll just mention a few lulus. Let's call them "Savage's Six Symbols of Stupidity":

- Byrd Green Bank Telescope
- Byrd Metals Fabrication Center
- Byrd Addition to the Lodge at Oglebay Park
- Byrd Hardwood Technologies Center
- Byrd Hilltop Office Complex

And now, my favorite (drum roll, please) . . .

- Byrd Institute for Advanced Flexible Manufacturing

Notice that there's no Robert C. Byrd Museum of African-American History. Or Robert C. Byrd Institute of Responsible Spending. We'll see a Ted Kennedy Institute for Aquatic Safety before we see those.

And still, this indefatigable rodent shows no sign of quitting—recently announcing that he will throw his hood into the ring in 2006.

Hasn't this country had enough of him?

It's time for the voters of West Virginia to gather their wits and set a trap for this creature. A lot of pork and a sensitive spring should be about all it takes. Yes, they should really replace that white hood with a pink slip and finally send this wretched little creature packing.

Jimmy Carter

Marxus peanutfarmera

JiMMY CaRTeR

[Marxus peanutfarmera]

The Big-Toothed Muskrat is a particularly nasty rodent that, while indigenous to the Southeastern United States, is known to appear as an endemic type in San Francisco, Boston, Manhattan, Austin, and as far north as Toronto, Canada (i.e. wherever socialists of the species gather). Though rarely productive in its first few stages of life, the Big-Toothed Muskrat is never sedentary and develops into more of a nuisance the older it gets. It is prone to attack fellow rodents to demonstrate its continued potency and destroys the natural balance of power in the ecosystem by inexplicably siding with vicious foreign predators against its own species. This rodent is never shrill, preferring to disarm his enemies with a non-display of his muted colors and feeds primarily on the praise of giant rats. A cunning beast, the Big-Toothed Muskrat will build an occasional shelter for other animals, at least when photographers are present. This way, when it helps steal what other animals have worked hard to forage, and disperses it to those animals too dull or slothful to forage for themselves, no one will question the muskrat's basic instincts. Mating for life, this critter bonds sexually with the opposite gender solely to reproduce, joining with the female of the species just once or twice in a lifetime.

Most people consider James Earl Carter good and decent. He doesn't drink. He doesn't gamble. He's been married to the same female for the past sixty years. And, unlike our most recent Democratic president, this Big-Toothed Muskrat doesn't even *smoke* cigars. As he told *Playboy* magazine so many years ago, the only place he's lusted is in his heart and certainly not in the small galley off the Oval Office. Besides, who would have him?

It's largely because of those qualities—highly unusual on the side of the forest where any permanent mating with a *female* is becoming newsworthy—that he was elected the thirty-ninth president of the United States.

Still, the fact that he is "good," "decent," and "married to the same mate for umpteen years" should not qualify him for the highest office in the land. If this were all it took to be elected president, I say we all vote for my nextdoor neighbor Carl in 2008. He's all of that, and more. He doesn't smoke, drink, or batter rabbits. Plus, he's tolerant. If all the other women in the world looked like Carl's wife Marge, Rosalynn Carter would be on *Baywatch*. Carl, bless his heart, calls Marge "his Italian bombshell," but it could be because of the pock marks on her face. In truth, she looks less like Sophia Loren than she does Danny DeVito. Though, to be fair, he's got better legs and is cleaner shaven.

Marge, however, does have a common touch. When she

becomes first lady, she'll replace Nancy Reagan's china with some good, old-fashioned U.S. Navy plates. That you can count on. So let's all get out and stump for neighbor Carl. He is a saint already. Let's make him president.

Carl would surely govern better than the pain from Plains. With the mighty muskrat at the helm, the United States was tossed into a tailspin of gross overspending, monumental inflation, and an oil and gasoline crisis that made even the post-Katrina madness seem like a bargain hunter's paradise.

But perhaps the Big-Toothed Muskrat's most ignominious contribution to history—if you don't count that recent Nobel Treason Prize—was his bungling of the Iran hostage crisis. By sanctimoniously undermining the Shah of Iran—am I being redundant, everything he has ever done has been sanctimonious—Carter threw open Tehran to the Ayatollah Khomeini, the first pustule in the ugly pox of Islamofascism now pandemic throughout the world. Shortly thereafter, a gang of hookah-puffing student fanatics sacked the American Embassy in Tehran and held our guys hostages for over fourteen months while the muskrat "malaised" away.

Perhaps the most intolerable effect of the crisis was that it led to the rise of Ted Koppel, the liberal spouting, socialist host of *Biteline* and ABC's answer to Alfred E. Newman. Today, of course, Koppel has thankfully retired to NPR (National Poverty Radio), though his hairpiece will still do an occasional appearance on ABC.

Fortunately, though, after Carter's interminable first term, Americans returned to their senses in time for the 1980 election and voted in no-nonsense Ronald Reagan by a landslide. This sent a clear message to Iran that the days of negotiation and failed rescue attempts in the desert were over. It's no coincidence that on the day of Mr. Reagan's inauguration, the hostages were finally released, having done more time than the average Massachusetts child rapist. What the mousy muskrat couldn't accomplish, the great Gipper could. The Left called it the "October Surprise," but after four years of Carter, any accomplishment would have surprised us all.

The Big-Toothed Muskrat showed his true colors— yellow and yellower—once again when only weeks after the seizing of the American embassy, Russia invaded Afghanistan. How did Carter respond? By forbidding U.S. athletes from participating in the 1980 Summer Olympic Games! Ooh, now that's playing hardball! *We're not going to stand by and let you overrun a defenseless country. We're going to punish you by letting you win more Gold Medals!* The Soviets were thrilled. Now, no one would even test the hormones of their female athletes. They could bring them back from the front. Talk about an overdose of Carter's Little Quiver Pills!

But the Big-Toothed Muskrat didn't suddenly become competent when he was drummed out of office in 1980. No, Carter, known in rapidly dwindling circles as "America's favorite ex-president" (which only means we're pleased as a Georgia peach that this toothy clodhopper is an "ex") has turned his misguided ambitions toward housing the world and making Third-World countries safe for dictatorships.

America was founded on the notion that hard work will pay dividends like the ownership of one's own home. But the King of Nuts thinks that *wanting* a home should count as much as working for one. And who does Gentleman Jimmy ask to support this foolishness? All of us industrious worker bees who spend the day pollinating our rears off so we can build our own hives.

Habitat for Humanity is the Marxist answer to self-sufficiency. It may be a hands-on project for a few do-gooders, but it is a hands-out project for the do-nothings. Jimmy Carter has become the Fidel Castro of government housing.

Most recently, this rodent, seemingly on a lifelong quest to atone for the errors of his presidency, has burrowed its way into the hearts and beards of dictators all across the globe. He's even proclaimed himself to be the fair-minded observer of political elections, near and far.

In 2004, the Venezuelan people held a recall vote,

designed to dump the Kook of Caracas, Landslide Hugo Chavez. Overseen by the Big-Toothed Muskrat, the election returns indicated a 59 percent to 41 percent victory for Chavez. The results were certified to be *fair and accurate* by Big Tooth and the little muskrats from the Carter Center, even though an independent exit poll conducted by an American firm indicated the *exact opposite results* against Chavez.

And although the Venezuelan electoral council was stacked with Chavez's stooges, Carter stood firm by his assertion of fairness. He didn't want to know that the electronic voting machines and software used for the election were provided by a Florida company, SmartMatic, owned by two Venezuelan suck-ups aligned with the guy whose hand is in the till, Landslide Hugo.

When two independent economists from Harvard and MIT analyzed the election data and found that there was a 99 percent likelihood that fraud ruled the outcome, the Big-Toothed Muskrat blew them off.

When the genocidal Palestinian Nazi gang Hamas won elections, Carter certified their win. This despite the fact that Hitler, too, won a democratic election.

And yet this chad-popping fraud of fairness still disputes the results of the 2000 U.S. presidential election. Unbelievable!

Hey, Big Tooth, it's time for you to trade your hammer

for a hammock! You've had a nice run. A lot longer than you deserve for starting the downhill slide this country is on. At the bottom of this slide isn't the smoothly groomed red clay of a peanut farm. It's the unforgiving sand of the Iraqi desert, and the shells in that part of the world are a good deal more ominous. Our soldiers face the greatest peril this country has encountered since the War for Independence, brought about by your support for the Ayatollahs and the spread of Islamic-terror.

So take those big muskrat teeth back to Plains. In Georgia, they know a varmint when they see one. They know treason when they see it, too. If you tried to launch a career today, you'd be more likely to be named King of Gaza or Imam of Syria than Sheriff of Chattahoochee County.

JaMeS CaRVilLe

[Canis trashi]

The K in K Street stands for kennel, and that's where the Dems keep this Junkyard Dog. Devotedly loyal to its masters, the Junkyard Dog's primary purpose is to attack anything that even smells Republican. One of the most unpleasant animals in the zoo and afflicted with a severe case of rabies, at least if the foam around the mouth is any indication, this species has shown a rare ability to crossbreed (with higher pedigreed poodles). That unlikely mating, however, has not eased this dirty dog's distemper, which flares up with great regularity.

"Junkyard" James Carville is a political animal of rare passion and divided loyalties. He developed a Louisiana accent, when there still was such a place, as thick as Governor Blanco's skull. Unlike her, however, he's not stuck on stupid. If Blanco had half his wit, Mayor Nagin's "Chocolate City" would still be chocolate. Heck, it would still be standing.

This Cajun has been ragin' in Democratic Party politics since he shepherded an unknown hound dog from Arkansas to the White House in 1992. During that campaign, the Junkyard Dog turned Fire Truck Dalmatian when it came to dousing flames, old and new, before they turned into full blown "bimbo eruptions." He attacked his work—and the bimbos—as only a mad dog can.

The Junkyard Dog, remember, is a *paid* political operative, an attack dog on a leash. Still, when you watch him on the Sunday morning talk shows, every now and then you can even catch a glimpse of nose-holding while he yelps about the virtues of the Democratic faith. Could this mutt actually have a conscience? Smart money says otherwise. Probably just caught a whiff of his own doggy breath.

If you give a dog the right treats, he'll bark up any tree. The Junkyard Dog is paid to hound his opponents whether they deserve it or not. And when his political masters set him loose on a target, he knows what his job is and how it has to be done.

As Clinton's attack dog, Carville was set loose on Paula Jones and any other *Lady* groped, fondled, propositioned, raped, or otherwise accosted by the *Tramp*, which meant half the population of the state. His handlers told the Junkyard Dog that nothing was out of bounds. We all remember his famous snarl, "Drag a hundred-dollar bill through a trailer park and there's no telling what you'll find." Well, drag a hundred-dollar bone down K Street, and there's no telling what you'll lure out of that moral waste site either.

The only thing more glaring than this dog's glower is his hypocrisy. After Newt Gingrich whipped the master strategist like a not-yet housebroken puppy in 1994, Clinton sicced the Junkyard Dog and his fellow hounds of war on Gingrich. The dog first bit into Gingrich's $4.5 million book deal, grabbed hold tight and wouldn't let go. With a straight face even, the Junkyard Dog called it unethical for a political official to profit from his office. He bayed on every major channel and half the minor ones, shredding the deal like an old newspaper. When Hillary Clinton pocketed her cool eight million dollars in a post-election book deal, however, the Junkyard Dog found nothing to bark about. And even if he had, the media would not have wanted to hear it.

The Junkyard Dog keeps one beady eye on the hand that feeds him, and another on the hand that's holding his leash. And in so doing, he proves again and again to be more two-faced than Cerberus, the three-headed hound from hell.

Despite his success in getting Clinton elected, in the post-Clinton era the Junkyard Dog still doesn't get to choose the company that he keeps or the causes he defends. When the Democratic Party wants him to shill for working poor, its masters spring the door of the mangy mutt's cage. He attacks Republicans as heartless thugs wanting to starve old people and roast black babies on open-flame spits. In the off-chance that you could ever get a word in edgewise to ask the dog how many seats the working poor had at the 2004 Democratic National Convention, you had better be prepared for him to come at your throat. Never mind that the teacher union educrats, labor thugs, abortion millers, and the Hate America First crowd manage the menagerie. What is important for the Junkyard Dog is whose lap he's paid to lie in.

Every now and then though, he forgets whose slippers he's supposed to fetch. The cycle usually begins when his shiny head has begun to swell, much like it did in the run-up to the 2004 election. Just two weeks before the election, the Junkyard Dog was heard telling a select group of Democratic elite: *"If we can't win this damn election with a Democratic Party more unified than ever before, with us having raised as much money as the Republicans, with 55 percent of the country believing we're heading in the wrong direction, with our candidate having won all three debates, and with our side being more passionate about the outcome than theirs—if we can't win this one, then we can't win shit! And we need to completely rethink the Democratic Party."*

We all know the punch line. Despite all their seeming advantages, the Democrats tanked. Then began the second phase of this old dog's cycle. Self-doubt. Within days of Kerry's defeat, Carville was circulating memos and growling to the media about his client's lack of a "defining narrative," not revealing, of course, that he was responsible for crafting that narrative. Bad dog.

But his Democratic masters will only tolerate so much ruckus in the kennel, and any pooch that dares to bite the hand that feeds it will eventually be left by the side of the road or taken to the pound. So we don't hear too much barking and yelping from inside the Junkyard Dog's cage anymore. As Shakespeare said, every dog has its day, and it seems that this yellow dog Democrat has already had his. It's time to put this Old Yeller back out on the Bayou.

Hugo Chavez
Thickheadus leninista

HuGo CHaVeZ

[Thickheadus leninista]

This cold-blooded and calculating amphibian is the largest and most deadly of South America's predators. Extremely poisonous, the Oily Armored Toad resembles a common frog, but gets its name for its preference to wallow in oil than swim in water, which explains its greasy appearance and its ability to slip out of tight situations. While its favored habitat is the expanse between the Andes and the Guiana Highlands, sandwiched between the Caribbean and the borders of Colombia and Brazil, the Armored Toad longs to strike out at territory in the north. Its mating habits are mostly unknown but most indications point to an excessive fetish for the almost-extinct island species, the *Cubanus dictatorum con beardus*. DANGER! This animal is not to be trusted and should be kept under constant surveillance!

Hugo "Oily Armored Toad" Chavez, the "elected" president of Venezuela, has made it perfectly clear that he hates America and its commitment to a free society. Well here's some news for you, Huey: We're not all that loco about you, either!

So what did we do to incur the Armored Toad's wrath?

It can't be our immigration policy. For years, we've opened our arms to countless shortstops from his opportunity-deficient backwater. And when these overpaid, overpampered jocks return home, their wallets overflowing with gringo cash and their necks weighted down with the latest and gaudiest American bling, Chavez seeks them out for photo ops. Then, when commending them for being such red-blooded all-Venezuelan boys, he conveniently forgets that these local heroes had to get their paws up to America to ply their otherwise irrelevant trade and then send the American greenbacks home so their families could survive.

And could we have possibly provided more pro-Venezuela airtime than that given to Ozzie Guillen, the jingoistic kiss-throwing manager of the Chicago White Sox? During the 2005 World Series, the Lizard of Oz would find the nearest camera, mouth his allegiance to Venezuela, and pound on his chest like King Kong.

No, what irks the deluded dictator is his belief that in 2002 the U.S. engineered the coup that ousted him from power for a total of three days! Take it from Dr. Savage, toad, if we had anything to do with it, you would've been gone a lot longer than seventy-two *horas*! In fact, you'd have been the *grenouille* on someone's plate before you could say, "Manuel Noreiga." Doubt us? Just ask "The Butcher of Baghdad" why he's now "The Crybaby of Cellblock D."

In blaming America, this toad conveniently overlooks the fact that there were plenty of people in his country who wanted to grease his skids and pronto. Why? Because as their president, he had deep-sixed the country's constitution and turned his nation into the kind of sorry Marxist enclave that only Harry Belafonte and Jimmy Carter could love.

The president of Colombia—another paragon of solid government—admitted in late 2005 that he gave asylum to seven Venezuelans who had confessed to planning and carrying out that short-lived coup. And they were plotting to do it again. And not an American among them. Go figure.

What's really ironic, though, is that this paranoid kook du jour was himself involved in a coup attempt in 1992. As a career army officer, he led a group of rebels trying to evict Venezuela's legally and constitutionally elected president, Carlos Andres Perez, who happened to be friendly toward the U.S. Unfortunately for this bungling bunch, they made every mistake possible and the Armored

Toad spent the next five-and-a-half years in an aquarium designed for toxic toads.

And yet, in keeping with the viral madness of Central and South American politics, and with some generous assistance from Jimmy Carter and the muskrats from the Carter Center, Chavez was elected president in 1998! What is it with the governments down there? Imagine the questionnaire for running for office:

Q: Have you ever held an elected post?
A: No.

Q: Do you have a history of civic involvement?
A: No.

Q: Do you like the United States?
A: No.

Q: Have you ever been in prison?
A: Si.

Q: Perfecto! When can you start?

I can see it now. When Enron's Ken Lay gets out of prison, he can move to South America, change his name to "Frito" Lay, take over Uruguay or Paraguay, and maybe even sell its power to California.

Still, although Chavez may be a joke, his presidency is no laughing matter. This is one toxic toad with more ambition than a frog ought to have. In addition to fast friend and mentor Fidel Castro, Chavez pals around with amphibious amigos Robert Mugabe of Zimbabwe, former Iranian President Khatami, and Kim Jong-Mentally-Il of Korea. He has become an active state sponsor of terrorism in South America and even hosts an Al Qaeda training facility on the Venezuelan island of—real name— "Margarita," an outward bound camp for wayward Muslim youth who want to work on their suntans and suicide bombings.

The Armored Toad is able to maintain his ill-gotten power by using rich oil deposits like a honey trap, around which the American Left predictably comes a-sniffing. In 2005, the trap snagged three Democratic Congressmen—Delahunt, Markey, and Serrano. The three shamelessly arranged for ten million dollars in discounted home heating oil for their districts from the Venezuelan-owned, U.S. subsidiary CITGO. Chavez announced the deal himself to embarrass the government that pays the congressmen's salaries.

Speaking of embarrassments, the Reverend Jesse Jackson was visiting this creature at the time of the announcement.

Now, there's a perfect pair. Two international toadies who blame America for every ill they've never suffered— from prejudice to political oppression to paper cuts incurred while collecting their endless stream of hand-outs.

Hey, forget the deposits. There's enough oiliness

between these slick reptiles to fuel the entire Western hemisphere.

Who cares that Amnesty International is investigating the Chavez government for murder and torture, and Human Rights Watch has denounced it for suppressing dissent? Not Harry Belafonte. "We're here to tell you," Harry told Chavez recently, "not hundreds, not thousands, but millions of the American people support your revolution." Jimmy Carter oversaw his election and declared it perfectly kosher.

These millions also include Belafonte and Cindy Sheehan, another suck up, and lots of other as yet unidentified people. Cindy must not know about Chavez's "Law on the Social Responsibility of Radio and Television," which criminalizes "insults, disrespect, and libelous remarks" aimed at the president with punishments up to forty months in jail. Cindy, honey, if you camp out in Chavez's front yard, be nice. You're in over your head in this frog's oil slick.

They really do play hardball down there.

DiCK CHeNeY

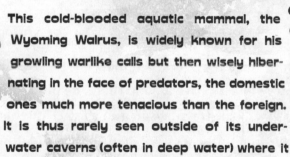

This cold-blooded aquatic mammal, the Wyoming Walrus, is widely known for his growling warlike calls but then wisely hibernating in the face of predators, the domestic ones much more tenacious than the foreign. It is thus rarely seen outside of its underwater caverns (often in deep water) where it hibernates and, liberal biologists believe, plans world domination. The Wyoming Walrus seems so menacing to weaker, herbivorous mammals—particularly donkeys and other asses—that few try to protect this species, and many in the eco-hybrid crowd have gone so far as to put a bounty on its head. A hardy mammal, indifferent to the environment—as is typical of breeds originating in states with no saltwater—crazed liberals believe the Wyoming Walrus actually welcomes oil spills and will sometimes swim in front of moving oil tankers hoping to get them to run aground (or so the media often reports). A free ranging carnivore, this slightly bloated specimen usually feeds on the carcasses of preening donkeys whose fatty heads clog up the Walrus's heart and arteries.

As we approach the aquatic exhibit, you'll notice the basso profondo growl of Dick Cheney, the Wyoming Walrus, one of the largest animals in the entire zoo, and also one of the meanest—at least according to the anti-walrus propaganda, which is legion. Yes, the Wyoming Walrus is definitely an animal with heart. After a string of heart surgeries beginning in 1978, this juggernaut now has a cardiac defibrillator to keep his allegedly cold, black heart pumping and to prevent us from having to face the prospect of a Vice President Hastert.

Liberal biologists say the Wyoming Walrus is the chief warmonger in the Bush administration. According to the more imaginative among them, he plotted with the unlikely combo of the Mossad and the FAA to open the skies for the 9/11 hijackers so that they could find their targets unimpeded. This was after having explosive charges placed in the basements of each tower so that they would ultimately collapse, which the walrus could then blame on the aircraft. The sad thing is that I am not kidding. Millions of people believe this. Oliver Stoned is making a 9/11 movie. Let's see who his bad guys are.

The Wyoming Walrus fits in naturally with the Republican herd. After all, the walrus and elephant have so much in common: a thick, tough hide for deflecting tough questions; ivory tusks for goring liberals; and (in the case of Bush) a congenital weakness for oil.

Though currently one of the most dominant species in

the zoo, the walrus got its start in politics as a pup in the office of an obscure Nixon administration official named Donald Rumsfeld. By the time Nixon left office in the wake of the Watergate scandal, Rumsfeld and Cheney were the only un-indicted Republicans left in Washington. This all but forced Gerald Ford to appoint Rumsfeld to White House chief of staff, and he brought Cheney along. There, both learned how not to be president. Before long, Rumsfeld made room for himself at the Department of Defense, and Cheney was promoted to White House chief of staff.

As Ford's campaign director in 1976, the ungainly walrus ran a better campaign than any walrus in history. But then again, walruses have no real history of running campaigns. Ford lost to Georgia Governor Jimmy Carter by two million votes. In 1992, he would steer George H.W. Bush's reelection campaign into that same pre-plowed ground, losing this time to Arkansas Governor Bill Clinton. What a record, Cheney's two candidates, incumbents both, lose to a pair of unknown rednecks. It's a good thing cousins Bo and Luke Duke didn't run against W and the Walrus in 2004. We'd have the Stars and Bars flying over the White House and cousin Daisy Duke playin' first lady. Campaign managing was obviously not Cheney's strong suit.

Unemployed, and without much in the way of prospects, the Wyoming Walrus turned his lonely eyes back home. There, he decided to run for Congress, the only state in which he could make up the entire state's delegation to the House of Representatives. As sole Wyoming congressman, he began to develop a taste for wider seas.

After many years away from the deep, the kinder and gentler Bush Senior sprung the Wyoming Walrus and let him loose in the White House once again, this time as secretary of defense.

In an odd twist of fate, actually not odd at all in the D.C. habitat, the Wyoming Walrus missed the Vietnam War only to oversee the 1991 Gulf War, proving that sometimes experience is not the best teacher at all. You'd have to be a Howard Dean or George Soros to find fault with the execution of that war. Unfortunately, the Dems have millions of Soros and Dean wannabes, whose lack of money and power makes them no less critical of every breath the Wyoming Walrus takes and indiscreetly hopeful that each breath will be the last.

Despite the Dems' manic criticism, Cheney has established the most effective model for a vice president—the wise, older, steadying hand without ambition—the exact opposite of Al Gore on every count. And though partial to cooler climes, the Wyoming Walrus has fended off some serious heat during Bush's second term. In the most elaborate of the imaginative scenarios, the walrus allowed the 9/11 hijackers to knock down the twin towers so that he would have an excuse to invade Iraq. Now since the lefties have convinced themselves that Saddam was no more threatening than Prince Rainier, they have to work their little brains to a frazzle to discover what possible reason we might have had for going to war. The problem is that they can't agree among themselves on a reason.

People like Joseph Wilson—and more on him later—say publicly that we did it to give Ariel Sharon license to oppress the Palestinians. Others think that it was done to enhance Bush's reelection chances. Many, of course, think it was for "oil," even though they have no idea how the oil thing works to our benefit. But the unifying field theory—the one that all of these wackjobs can subscribe to at least in small part—is "Halliburton," the now almost mythical company the Wyoming Walrus once headed.

Here's how it works: Cheney invoked a national catastrophe and launched a difficult war so a company he once worked for could get a cost-plus-two-percent contract to reconstruct Iraq under extraordinarily dangerous circumstances. As the Left now revises our history books, expect to see Halliburton credited with the Korean War, the War of 1812, and the Peloponnesian War as well.

The Wyoming Walrus also finds himself implicated in the most preposterous non-scandal in Washington history. Let's see, the preening "ambassador" Joseph Wilson conspires with his CIA wife to go to Africa. Wilson lies about his wife's involvement, lies about who sent him, lies about what he found, lies about to whom he reported—allegedly Cheney himself—and becomes a media darling. When the walrus's chief of staff, Scooter Libby, un-tells Wilson's lies, Libby gets investigated. My favorite detail: Wilson shares with *Vanity Fair* the fact that wife Valerie Plame outed herself as a top secret CIA agent on their *third* date during "a heavy make-out session." Says the coy Wilson, "It did nothing to dampen my ardor." Thanks for sharing.

But all of this uproar now seems a distant memory as the Wyoming Walrus's ultimate legacy will unfortunately involve a bizarre hunting mishap. On February 11, 2006, Cheney was hunting quail (the bird, not Bush Sr.'s vice president) on a private Texas ranch, and accidentally sprayed his hunting companion, Harry Whittington, with birdshot. Whittington, a seventy-eight-year-old Austin attorney, could not have been more gracious about the accident, not faulting Cheney in the least and putting up a brave face for the media. But the media was not so forgiving. They quickly declared open season on the Wyoming Walrus and hunted and fired at their quarry with less discretion than Cheney himself, trying desperately to use a tragic accident to define this walrus's otherwise exemplary tenure.

And so the Wyoming Walrus has promised not to run for president in 2008, which is especially good now, since he needs the break. As vice president, lumbering through the dark corridors of the White House, pushing the buttons and fighting the worst fascists since Hitler's Nazis, he has already gone beyond the call of duty, a duty made all the rougher when you've got a seditious media praying—to the degree that they remember how—that you'll gore yourself with your own tusks.

Jacques Chirac

Frogus europenis

JaCQueS CHiRaC

[*Frogus europenis*]

This unsightly, mutated Le Lézard is actually an interspecies descendent of the frog and chicken. Although both of its progenitors are vertebrates, something bad happened in the crossbreeding as this creature shows absolutely no trace of a backbone. A more telling trait is that when exposed to a frightening situation, Le Lézard's natural response is to change his color most often to red or yellow. In his native country, this reptile has earned the nickname *Chameleon Bonaparte.*

Jacques Chirac (rhymes with "Iraq") has been the president of France since 1995. Because of a quirk in the French Constitution—the document, not their fortitude, they having none—the president has control over two areas: foreign policy and the military.

I know what you're thinking. In charge of the French military? Besides being president of the Maurice Chevalier Fan Club, could there possibly be any position of lesser power? Hasn't the French army been waxed more often than Madonna's lucky star? Well, yes, actually. And that brings us to Le Lézard's second realm of responsibility: foreign policy, an area where this nimble politico changes positions as frequently as a Rue St. Germaine hooker.

In his second run for president of the republic in 2002, Le Lézard promised strong punishment for crime and for terrorism. Did I hear right, or did somebody stick a croissant in my ear? Le Lézard, strong on terrorism? What a load of crepe!

Let's review here: this mix-breed son of a frog and chicken campaigns that he's anti-terrorist. And yet, when some smelly, deranged clowns, who have somehow misdialed Allah, fly death planes into our buildings, he turns his other French-kissed cheek? If those slime molds weren't terrorists, what were they? Lost? Directionally challenged?

But when our bandaged and bruised country inexplicably gets on its knees to make nice with the U.N. (Useless Negotiators), Le Lézard pledges to veto any resolution that would support our going after the terrorist-breeding regime that cheered when we got sucker-punched and lost over 3,300 American lives.

And this Jacques-ass says he's anti-terrorism?

Has this galling Gaul forgotten that we're the ones who liberated his useless little republic from the stranglehold of Nazism? We suffered over 6,000 casualties on D-Day alone so his country of Prozac-popping snots could live in freedom. And what does he give us in return? A French kiss-off.

So where is Le Lézard coming from? How could he turn his back on us? Well, read on, folks, because once again, it is my pleasure to help you become a Savage Savant.

It all started in 1974, when the vice president of Iraq, a pockmarked yellow fellow named Saddam Hussein, invited the French prime minister (not the president) to Baghdad. And who was this French P.M. who visited Iraq, and soon thereafter began calling Saddam Hussein "bon ami"? You got it...Jacques-o! And to date, he's the only Western leader to have had personal interaction with the thankfully imprisoned despot.

But there's a whole lot more to this French connection. It was not long after Le Lézard's visit that Saddam approved a deal granting French oil companies a number of privileges...plus a 23 percent share of Iraqi oil. Mmmm, you could cook a heckuva lot of *coq au vin* with that oil!

Then, published reports indicate, Le Lézard okayed a deal to sell two reactors to Iraq—a one-megawatt research reactor and a seventy-megawatt reactor—along with enough uranium to produce several nuclear devices. By the late 1970s, only one country supplied more civilian and military equipment to Iraq—none other than the terrorist-nurturing Mother Russia. And so the freaks from France and their Russian comrades supplied Hussein with whatever armaments he desired. Happily, the Israelis decided that this was a toy Saddam was not yet ready to play with, and they took it away. Took it out actually.

And people wonder where all those WMD rumors came from.

So, are you getting a picture of why France was not so eager to get into the fray against Iraq? Are you beginning to see why Jacques and his jackals might not want to bite the unwashed hands that feed them? And we haven't even gotten to the billions in oil-for-food money that the French were pocketing. No, Saddam was their best customer. And with California making better wine, Wisconsin making better cheese, and the Scandinavians making better porn—or at least porn with better looking girls—the French had to sell something to someone.

Well, such duplicitous policies have nevertheless come back to bite Chameleon Bonaparte. And not on the hand either. No, Le Lézard's indecisions are coming back to bite him in the derriére.

Just take a look at "les emeutes" that erupted this past November. Wanting to have a cook out, and realizing that hamburgers and hot dogs were against their religion, the Muslim youth cooked automobiles instead, more than eight thousand of them in every major metro in France. Meanwhile, the shellacked lizard-man crawled into a hole for over six weeks, paralyzed with inaction!

Now, rewind the scene to a year earlier. When the Simon Wiesenthal Center appealed to the French president in November 2004 to clamp down on anti-Semitic organizations linked to terrorist organizations, like Hamas, Le Lézard couldn't be bothered. In a repeat of the old French tradition of "Let them eat cake," Le Lézard instead sent his lackey-in-chief, Dominique de Villepin (Dominique Détente), to respond by saying that they had already cracked down by questioning a hundred Islamic radicals. Sure, that'll stop them.

Of course, by that time, the police had all but abandoned many areas around Paris because of the armed Islamic gangs that controlled "les banlieus." These suburbs are occupied by most of the North African immigrants that make up 10 percent of France's population.

The French put the Muslims out there because they didn't want them messing up their inner cities. Out of sight out of mind, they figured. It didn't quite work out that way.

During the recent riots, Le Lézard's main concern was to protect not the citizenry, but France's cherished multicultural image. As habitual shade-shifters, chameleons have to accept people of all colors, even though Le Lézard is almost always a pale shade of yellow (at least on his belly) to blend in with his European cohorts.

So instead of arresting rioters, Le Lézard ordered the imprisonment of some of the police officers that had been videotaped controlling rioters with batons! That's right. In the middle of the largest security crisis since the 1968 riots, Le Lézard employed his favorite technique (one he's used on numerous occasions) and alienated his biggest ally: the police who were trying to restore order and calm to the cities.

When it dawned on Le Lézard after several weeks of escalating violence that the situation was serious, he finally invoked emergency police powers granted to the government by the French Constitution. The damage, though, had been done. And the chameleon had finally shown its true color: transparent.

Once order had been restored, Le Lézard, in the spirit and very words of Jimmy Carter, promised to address the "profound malaise" amongst the Muslim population. In other words, he intended to throw some money at the problem and hope it went away at least until after his next *vacances*. As is true to the lizard's bold style, he made no mention of outlawing terrorist groups or breaking up the Islamic gangs.

One economist has estimated that France has already spent $40 billion since 2000 to address the problem, with no indication that more money would do anything but reward people for burning cars. Le Lézard's stunning indifference, incompetence, and collaborationist tendencies give new meaning to Hitler's question asked during World War Two: "Is Paris burning yet?"

Paris may not be burning, but France is truly cooked. Even Dr. Savage sees no way out of this one. At least our illegals aren't Muslims. Theirs are. The French can't integrate them and will not deport them, and they are about the only people in the country having babies. Bonne chance, Lizard Man. Unlike 1944, we're too busy pulling the knives out of our backs to come to save your sorry derriére this time.

If I were you, I would just crawl back under the rock you crawled out from and hope it all goes away.

BillClinton

Fondlem undgropeum

BiLL CLiNTON

[*Fondlem undgropeum*]

The Celebrated Arkansas Werewolf is so entirely distinct that there is nothing or no one quite like it in captivity or in the wild. Wolf Boy, as he is sometimes called given his failure to grow up and become an adult of any species, is native to the Southeastern United States, but now roams the world in a pack of one. His mother, Virginia, was a human; that much is known. His lupine nature he derives from his father, about whom nothing is known. Wolf Boy has received international attention as the most outsized, most outrageous, most entertaining animal in the zoo. His indiscreet and indiscriminate mating rituals and borderline criminal activities have captivated the media and the masses for years. Do not be fooled, though, for this semi-lupine wonder is one of the zoo's most dangerous inhabitants. Wolf Boy was put on the endangered species list after Waco, after Whitewater, after Troopergate, after Travelgate, after Filegate, after Chinagate, after Monica and his subsequent impeachment, after Pardongate, and the pillaging of the White House, but seemingly not even a cross held before his very eyes can stop his marauding. Wolf Boy is occasionally seen stalking the streets of Harlem or in the New York countryside or reportedly in Ireland, whose clueless population has only seen the boy part and not the wolf. He tries to keep a full hemisphere away from the one creature of whom he is justly petrified, the Limber Leopard of Chappaqua with which he once mated.

As we near the habitat of this unique creature, Bill "Wolf Boy" Clinton, a word of warning: Men, hold close your wives. And your daughters. And your granddaughters. And your grandmothers. And their mothers. And their mother's mothers. And remember, neither your cane nor your walker offers any discouragement when Wolf Boy is excited. And please, ladies, whatever you do, don't wear blue. The color alarms him, arouses him, and triggers memories that are not all good.

Men, as crude as this may sound, the graves of your loved ones are not exactly safe either when Wolf Boy is on the prowl. "You know," Wolf Boy reportedly said in 1996 upon seeing an Incan mummy on display at a National Geographic Museum, "if I were a single man, I might ask that mummy out. That's a good-looking mummy." Not being single, he had to content himself with sexual assault. Oh, would that we were joking!

Remember when Wolf Boy first entered the White House? We thought he had promised us "the most ethical administration in history," but we obviously misunderstood. He meant the "most comical." Said Wolf Boy after leaving office, "I may not have been the greatest president, but I've had the most fun eight years." Again, we wish we were joking.

His was less of a presidency, really, than a French farce. Or a circus. Yes, if the world of politics is a zoo, then the Clinton administration was the circus, an outrageous, audacious parade of amazing illusions and death-defying acrobatics, with the amazing Wolf Boy as both the ringmaster and the star freak of the sideshow.

We all remember this creature's most infamous routines, all the various "Gates," the women in the Oval office, the bodies in the park, the Red Chinese in the parlor, the furniture in Chappaqua, the sundry waggings of the dog.

Clinton collected scandals like other men collect stamps and his didn't come pre-licked: Monica Lewinsky. Susan McDougal. Paula Jones. Gennifer Flowers. Kathleen Willey. Juanita Broaddrick. Some were willing, some were apparently not, but from his perspective—and the media's—it didn't matter. Wolf Boys will be Wolf Boys, or so we were told, and the sexual harassment rules that he helped write took a holiday, at least for him.

And let's not forget the sly Wolf Boy's historic improv lines, classics all: "It depends on how you define *alone*," or, "I experimented with marijuana a time or two, and I didn't like it. I didn't inhale and never tried it again," or better still, "It depends on what the meaning of the word *is* is." More bizarre still, his supporters admired, and still do, his ability to dance on the head of a semantic pin. They see in that, his, as well as their, superior Blue State intellect.

If Wolf Boy slipped, which he did often, the media made sure they did not have to hear it. In the 2000 State of the Union speech, he said, "Last year, the vice president launched a new effort to help make communities more liberal." He meant "livable," yet he repeated this Freudian error in the next sentence. Of course, the networks deep-sixed that one, but those of us who were watching enjoyed every preposterous minute of it.

For a talk radio guy, Wolf Boy's secretions were like manna from heaven. Every day there was something new. The so-called scandals today don't begin to measure up. Oh my, there is a lobbyist in the White House! In Wolf Boy's day there were Red Chinese gunrunners in the White House. Oh, there is collateral damage in Tikrit! In Wolf Boy's reign, there was collateral damage in Waco, Kosovo, and Serbia!

How long do you think Bush would have survived a tank assault on a religious community inhabited largely by minorities—twenty-eight of them black—that resulted in the burning death of twenty children and sixty others? How long would Bush have survived an armed assault on a minority community and the extrication of a six-year-old at the business end of an assault rifle to be shipped off to communist Cuba? How long would Bush have survived an undeclared, unannounced, unapproved-by-anyone war that we were told was because of 100,000 Kosovars in mass graves when less than a thousand dead Kosovars were ever found? How long would Bush have survived the death of his most popular black cabinet member in an "inexplicable" plane crash and an autopsy-less burial after a seeming bullet hole had been found in his head?

Those who know the Wolf Boy era know that I am just scratching the surface—Grand Escalante anyone? Mena? Castle Grande? TWA Flight 800? VAAPCON? John Doe #2? In some ways, I miss the strange days and stranger ways of Wolf Boy. Don't we all yearn for the TGIF afternoons, when the White House attack machine would dump the newest bit of scandal—just in time to get buried in the weekend news cycle? Entertaining days, indeed.

And the comedic careers that Wolf Boy launched, all the dancing bears, trained seals, squawking parrots, and other sideshow freaks—James Carville, Joe Lockhart, Paul Begala, John Podesta, George Stephanopoulos, Sid Blumenthal, Anne Lewis, Barney Frank, the two Lanis. Bush has given us no such comic relief. Nothing close.

Where would America be today without these improv superstars? They raised the arts of spin, attack, and stonewall to levels not seen since Goebbels hit the slab.

To be sure, the Wolf Boy and the Limber Leopard slunk out of town dragging the china and furniture in the U-Haul behind them. That was fun, almost as much fun as when the co-presidents poured a flurry of last minute pardons on us—no, a veritable *blizzard* of pardons: in-laws, outlaws, Puerto Rican terrorists, child molesters, international rapscallions. The world had not seen such an outpouring of bad characters since the anthrax scare cleared the Senate building.

Among my personal favorite pardons were that laughable pair, Carlos "the Nose" Vignali, convicted cocaine kingpin, and Almon "Deadbeat" Blaswell, notorious tax cheat. Within a month of his pardon, Deadbeat was under investigation again for tax evasion. These two got off with the help of Hillary's half-brother, Hugh Rodham.

Among the 140 pardons issued on that last day, one went to Wolf Boy's slapstick little salamander of a brother, Roger "Hoover" Clinton, and another to vaudeville king, Marc Rich. His fugitive act got more than a little grease from his ex-wife, Denise Rich, who made several large and timely contributions to the Democratic National Committee. A month later, Rich was said to be back to his old tricks serving as middleman for illegal Iraqi oil sales. These were real scandals, guys! By the Clinton White House standards, Jack Abramoff is a reformer.

But the Wolf Boy, who kept America in stitches and our defense lawyers in high cotton, has moved on to greener pastures. Upon whom could this aging predator now possibly be preying? With so much time on his lupine paws, how does he stay out of trouble? Sure, he can go to

Africa and pontificate about AIDS, but those of us who follow such things know that he has much to atone for.

Just last year, the Canadian press broke a chilling story: In the early 1980s, Wolf Boy, while still governor, awarded a contract to Health Management Associates to care for the state's prisoners. Needless to say, the president of the company ran with Wolf Boy's pack. As part of the deal, HMA also collected the prisoners' blood for eventual sale. With AIDS exploding in the U.S., the prisoners' blood proved unsellable—here at least. So HMA laundered it through some middlemen, and it ended up in Canada. Last year, the Canadian Red Cross accepted responsibility for distributing the HMA blood and the three thousand AIDS and Hepatitis C related deaths it caused. Author Michael Galster, who did medical work in the Arkansas prison system, traced the "Blood Trail" to Wolf Boy, whom he claims knew all about it and may have gotten a cut.

As fond as they had grown of Canada, the American media were still much fonder of Wolf Boy and killed the story deader than its victims. So Wolf Boy's career lived for another day, but to what end? Surely he's got to be into something sneaky, like selling nuclear secrets to China or building nuclear power plants for North Korea or diddling Miss World. Wait, been there, done all of that.

Now we're even starting to hear about the Clinton

legacy, perhaps the most entertaining burlesque of all. To help get the party started, Wolf Boy turned his attention to building a brand-new funhouse—the William Jefferson Clinton U.S. Presidential Library and Double Wide. There we learn how, like a modern day Houdini, he single-handedly balanced the federal budget. The words "under Republican pressure" never appear. Nor do the phrases "raising taxes" or "slashing defense spending" or "letting Al Qaeda enjoy an intelligence-free field day."

Last year, we discovered that his own legacy wasn't the only one to get Wolf Boy thinking. At the funeral of Pope John Paul II, he generously volunteered the Pope "may have had a mixed legacy . . . there will be debates about him." But in none of these debates will we hear the words "blue dress," "obstruction of justice," "tainted blood," or "wag the dog." (Oh, yes, remember that Sudanese aspirin plant!)

Wolf Boy then took his dog and pony show on the road with former president and George H.W. Bush to raise support for the survivors of the Indian Ocean tsunami. Like an awkward Martin and Lewis reunion, those two geezers yukked it up all over Asia with Wolf Boy's Asian dialect parodies and pick-up lines adding spice to the otherwise morbid proceedings.

And so this sideshow freak continues to spread his mischief, most recently barking outrageous statements regarding the outbreak of violence surrounding the infamous Dutch cartoons that satirized Muslims. Yes, Wolf Boy hit a new low after the "cartoon riots" by urging the socialists in the E.U. to arrest and convict the cartoonists who caricatured Mohammed! No punishment for the murderers, or rioters. And this is what passes for a "progressive" or a "liberal" today! Neo-fascism is loose and the Clintons lead the wolf pack.

So why, you ask, isn't Dr. Savage laughing at the outrageous gags of the high-flying, death-defying Wolf Boy? Because beneath all the shtick, all the captivating performances, all the yuks and the tricks of this clever creature, lies the cold-blooded heart of a wolf.

And before he is through, he will strike again. Watch your back. The darkest nightmare scenario being the leopard as president, the wolf at the U.N. As the sign read in Scarface, "The World Is Yours." Let's pray it does not appear in neon above the White House.

Hillary Clinton
Peronista manipulatus

HiLLaRY CLINToN

[Peronista manipulatus]

The Limber Leopard, an agile and extremely dangerous member of the cat family, is native to the Great Lakes but adapted surprisingly well to the remote areas along Arkansas' Whitewater River.

As the queen of her species, this thick-legged predator is known for her domination of the pack, and her one advantage is being able to change her spots at will. This sturdy animal is also known for the unusual processes she uses for selecting a breeding partner. Although she may appear asexual, this predatory beast has a keen eye for the Alpha Male of her species, or at least one that she could hector into seeming like an Alpha Male. Although the Limber Leopard tolerates the Alpha's sexual waywardness, she can become entirely vicious towards any female of the species that threatens the Alpha status of her mate.

The former first lady and current junior senator "from New York," Hillary Clinton, is up for reelection in 2006, a senatorial race that many see as a cakewalk. (Assuming her husband doesn't gorge himself on the cake first.) The predicted victory in 2006 will, according to the Washington rumor mill, give her the inside track on the 2008 Democratic presidential nomination.

Heaven, help us.

Although she's quite cagey about expressing her desire for the presidency, the Limber Leopard gets very touchy when asked about her qualifications. In her 2000 Senate campaign, this big cat constantly yelped about her thirty years of professional political experience, which began, amazingly, as volunteer organizer for Barry Goldwater's presidential campaign. Imagine a teenage Tom DeLay handing out Ralph Nader literature, and you have some sense of the incomprehensibility of this.

This feline also purred about the valuable professional experience she gained in her eight years as "co-conspirator," or rather "co-president."

Co-presidency? Yes, you remember what she said in 1992: "If you vote for my husband, you get me; it's a two-for-one, blue plate special." While she boasted of two-for-ones, hubbie was thinking more about two-on-ones. Granted, the Limber Leopard knows her way around the Oval Office—although not nearly as well as a few dozen other women from that era (it was, after all, affectionately known as the Oral Office under Bill). According to some insiders, she would often sit at the president's desk day dreaming of fulfilling her political fantasy. Given her husband's predilections, perhaps she didn't spend enough time under that desk fulfilling his fantasies. Yes, the embarrassing procession of bimbos starting, at least publicly, with Gennifer Flowers and climaxing with (and all over) Monica Lewinsky gave new meaning to the phrase *executive privilege.*

During her White House years, the "frost lady" tackled some mind-boggling issues—none more ill-conceived than her approach to national healthcare. Her 1,300-page overhaul proposal was as convoluted as a cow's intestines. And deceptive. While bashing the insurance companies on the one hand, four of the industry leaders—Aetna, Cigna, Met Life, and Prudential—helped design the scheme.

Thankfully, when it turned out that the leopard's pride was guarding the gazelles, the prey turned on the predator. With her policies threatening to turn Department of Motor Vehicles branches into doctors' offices, Americans decided that they didn't want this "co-president" in charge of their health decisions. In 1994, her brazen overstep provoked voters to foist full congressional control—the Dems lost an incredible fifty-four House and eight Senate seats—on the opposition. Almost single-pawedly, the Limber Leopard switched a Democratic Congress to a Republican one. All in all, it was the biggest first-lady PR bungle since Mary Todd Lincoln overspent her decorating budget on wallpaper and chintzes in wartime.

Then too, some other shenanigans from the First Leopard didn't help much either. Travelgate, Filegate, Cattlegate, Whitewater, and Vince Foster come quickly to mind. And these are just the tip of the ice queen.

Not that our feline friend hasn't done more to embarrass herself. In 1996, the Limber Leopard launched a campaign to build relationships with Muslim groups, including the Council on American-Islamic Relations (CAIR) and the American Muslim Council (AMC)—organizations you might call front groups for the child-killers of Hamas, the Palestinian terrorist organization. These groups held a conference in 1998, where speakers called for jihad and labeled Jews as "pigs and monkeys." (Ah, the compassionate face of liberalism. It's a good thing she's not associating with those intolerant, bigoted conservatives.)

After the invasion of Afghanistan, she wrote an op-ed about the importance of restoring women's rights in the oppressive country. "She cannot defend her own rights against her husband," said Gen. Suhaila Siddiq, the nation's only female general. "How can she defend the rights of my country?" Good question.

And what about when, following the 9/11 tragedy, the Hillarious One spearheaded a federal government relief package of $21.4 billion, the passage of which she called the proudest moment of her life. That's other people's money, hon. You don't get to heaven by giving it away. (Bush did the same in New Orleans, which is why Savage sees our government as an oligarchy of Demicans and Republicrats.)

A four-month investigation by the *New York Daily News* found that most of the money had been squandered and virtually no funds went for actual 9/11-related expenses. Oh well. Of course, the Limber Leopard just responded in typical liberal fashion: She asked for another twenty billion. Maybe she can hire Ken Lay to make sure it's accounted for properly.

It's not that she doesn't have some truly important qualifications for political office. She does, for instance, know how to speak out of all four sides of her face. In her bid to become the first female president in 2008, the leopard has experimented with more positions than Bill and Gennifer.

For the anti-war crowd, our spot-changing senator says she's for a pull out of Iraq.

For the pro-war crowd, she stands by her congressional vote to support the war.

For the liberal crowd, she's supportive of Muslim interests.

For the conservative crowd, she supports a protective barrier for Israel.

And then there are these moderate morsels dropped in her leopard stew—advocacy against violent video games and support for a ban on flag burning.

She's serving more sides than a short-order cook.

Far from her days of supporting (and springing) Puerto Rican terrorists, the Limber Leopard is even trying to come off as hardnosed on illegal immigration. She's criticized the Bush administration for not doing more to stem the tide and for short-changing INS frontline workers. Naturally, she forgot to mention that she and Chuck Schumer voted against funding for two thousand more border patrol agents and five thousand additional detention beds to end the INS's catch-and-release policies. But, hey, what's a little selective memory when you're trying to take over the world?

The Limber Leopard's mastery of public policy issues doesn't seem to have an end. The indictment of her 2000 Senate campaign finance chairman shows how well she understands campaign finance reform.

Perhaps her most important quality, however, is something Tricky Dick Nixon saw in her shortly before he died. Back when President Clinton was willy-nilly about bombing Bosnia and Serbia, Nixon said that all of this indecisiveness reflected poor leadership from one Clinton, but not the other.

Indeed, on January 19, 1999, having just barely survived impeachment, the president touched on the subject of Kosovo two-thirds of the way into his typical State of the Union stem winder. He spent forty-three words, just slightly more than he needed to seduce Monica (including the call for a pizza).

Then, someone in that White House persuaded the president that America needed its Alpha Male to start acting like one, and not just in the back galley of the Oval Office. The message apparently sunk in.

Two months later—without consulting Congress, the U.N., or the American people—we were bombing the life out of civilian Serbia. (The Serbian military effectively protected its planes and tanks from "our" NATO bombers!) Over the course of the next ten weeks, "NATO aircraft" most of them ours—flew more than thirty-eight thousand combat missions, killing thousands of Serbs and destroying just about every bridge over the Danube (not shown on any news outlet!). To justify the war, the Clinton administration promised we'd find literally hundreds of thousands of Kosovars in mass graves. According to the U.N. itself, the final count was about six hundred, the kind of numbers—and the kind of killing also—that you'd get in a year's worth of L.A. gang wars. "When Clinton lied, no one died," some say. Tell that to the Serbs.

No sweat, though. A supplicant media had no more interest in these deaths than the ones in Arkansas—or Fort Marcy Park for that matter.

But despite the media's incessant cheerleading and whitewashing of the Limber Leopard's ascension, Hillary squandered her only chance to establish herself as a serious candidate for the presidency. In a blistering attack on President Bush in January 2006, she said the president had "outsourced" the diplomacy with regard to Iran. This is, of course, an outlandish and absurd statement. Was Hillary stating that she did not want diplomacy? Was she suddenly stating that everything she screamed for prior to the Iraq War (i.e. go to the U.N. and to the European Union and "give peace a chance") suddenly was not a policy she approved of? Was Hillary suddenly saying that by "outsourcing" diplomacy on Iran—by taking the moderate course—that President Bush was doing the wrong thing? Was she suggesting that Iran be bombed immediately? In doing so, this bloodthirsty predator showed that she is a craven politician without the balance necessary for the important job of the presidency.

Still, the Limber Leopard is a dangerous breed, one that Richard Nixon said "inspires fear." Yes, we should all be a little afraid, very afraid. This leopard may change her spots, but she's not about to change her nature.

George Clooney
Blando whiskerus

GEORGE CLOONEY

[Blando whiskerus]

This Cheshire Cat is a smooth yet deceptively dangerous breed that makes use of its natural talent to pretend to be something that its not, although never quite convincingly. The Cheshire Cat has become a favorite pet on the Left Coast where one can build a career on a charming smile. The Cheshire Cat's empty-headed philosophizing and its magical ability to appear and disappear at will are also useful virtues in a hookah-smoking Wonderland where ex-wives and narcotics cops are on the prowl. "A grin without a cat!" said Alice of the disappearing Cheshire. "It's the most curious thing I ever saw in all my life!"

More kitty litter than cool cat, George Clooney is, at first glance, a seemingly intelligent, happy-go-lucky friend to man. But don't be fooled by his pasted-on smile and perpetual, roguish five o'clock whiskers.

Beware: This schizophrenic alley-cat can turn faster than Siegfried and Roy's tigers, who are distant—but more benign—relatives.

If in Texas, they say "all hat and no cattle", in Hollywood, it's all smile and no gray matter. The Cheshire Cat has never had an original idea of his own, but he can regurgitate political hairballs quicker than you can say, "Why are you investigating me?"

That is the line from the movie *Syriana* that you have heard a thousand times on the TV trailer. The Cheshire Cat starred in the movie and served as executive producer. *Why are you investigating me*, indeed?

Why? Well, there is a story here, a curious one. The movie is based on the book *See No Evil* written by former CIA agent Bob Baer, whom Clooney plays in the movie. In the book, and in real life, the "you" was the Clinton administration, which was investigating Baer because he resisted the effort of the Democratic National Committee to secure a White House security clearance for Clinton donor Roger Tamraz, an international rapscallion and possible front man for the KGB.

With the Cheshire Cat at the helm, however, the time frame of the movie somehow shifts from the totally corrupt 1996 presidential campaign—the subject of the book—to the present day. And although the movie does not mention George W. Bush by name, it might as well have. The bad guys in this movie are Texas oilmen yanking the chain of a corrupt American president. The good guys are the movie's suicide bombers.

This fraudulent film was honored with the "Modern Master Award" at the Santa Barbara International Film Festival. And in a beautifully karmic moment, when Clooney held the prize over his head, the trophy broke into pieces and fell to the floor. Could there possibly be a better symbol for the cheap tactics and shoddy talent of this so-called modern master?

His movie, *Good Night and Good Luck*, was at least as dishonest as *Syriana*. In this movie, written in pitch perfect parlor pink patois, the "evil" Joe McCarthy targets two real life people, both innocent, and presumably destroys them. In real life, however, McCarthy had nothing to do with Air Force Lieutenant Milo Radulovich, who was exonerated anyhow. He did target Annie Lee Moss, but she worked in the Code Room of the Pentagon and was in fact a Soviet agent. Even the Cheshire Cat wouldn't hire a member of Al Qaeda to work in the code room today, let alone his editing room, and Al Qaeda isn't half the threat that the Soviets were back then. So what's the point, Cheshire? As Alice learned, with the Cheshire Cat, that's just it. In Wonderland, there is no point.

In the Wonderland of Hollywood, however, there is no one who knows enough to tell the Cheshire Cat much of anything besides what a great smile he has. This has surely gone to his head—there is room aplenty in it—and may explain why the Cheshire Cat appeared at the G8 summit in Scotland last summer to hawk more money for African dictators. Apparently, they needed to replenish their funds for new AK-47s and miscellaneous torture devices.

And what else could have led Clooney to offer the following insight when a reporter from the *London Observer* asked him about America's post-9/11 military actions? "We [Americans] don't understand that people actually get mad at us. We still think of ourselves in terms of WW2," said the cat, grinning. "The problem is that the world has changed, and our involvement in these tiny places is different than it was in 1941. It was a lot clearer then. We were attacked."

That's right, folks. According to The Madness of King George, things are different now, because back in 1941, we were attacked. I know what you're thinking. "What? We weren't attacked on 9/11?" Not in the Cheshire Cat's world of unreality. You see, Karl Rove and Osama bin Laden got together and planned to rev up the American war machine to boost the economy and steal Middle Eastern oil. In fact, this feline went so far as to say, "Bin Laden didn't come from the abstract. He came from somewhere, and if you look where . . . you'll see America's hand of villainy."

Yes, the sinister President Bush secretly moved the World Trade Towers into the path of those peace-loving Al Qaeda flying enthusiasts as part of an international set-up.

This is the Wonderland that Left Coast liberals live in. "Curiouser and curiouser" to be sure.

You know, there's a reason why *Premiere* magazine doesn't release a "50 Sexiest Politicians" issue (with Hillary Clinton landing somewhere around 782). Likewise, there's an even better reason why no one should ever listen to or care anything about what any of these boob-enhanced Botoxed buffoons have to say about politics.

Perhaps having made the movie *Three Kings* set during the Persian Gulf War, the Cheshire Cat now considers himself a military analyst and strategist. But the point of *Three Kings*, made while Clinton was still president, is that we were wrong to leave Iraq before we booted the bad guys out. Do I remember right? Yes, I do. Here's the plot summary from International Movie Data Base: "[Clooney and pals] learn that the civilians have been encouraged by the U.S. government to rise up and fight Sadaam Hussein, but are facing certain execution because the U.S. military refuses to help them. This incident creates a crisis of conscience for the American soldiers."

"The U.S. military refuses to help them," can you believe that? The nerve of our military not intervening in Iraq when the people needed us.

Curioser and curiouser!

But you see, folks, the truth is that the Cheshire Cat is really only an expert in one area.

What is that, you ask?

I'll give you a hint. It starts with a B and ends with an S.

Just recall his failed attempt as a television producer on the thankfully short-lived HBO series, *K Street*. Set in Washington D.C., it featured a lobbying firm run by the real-life political—and stranger-than-life—couple, Mary Matalin and James Carville (or, as they're known in the Savage Nation: "Booty and the Beast"). Cheshire envisioned this as a program that would show the bare-knuckle world of political hardball. But what appeared was a game of liberal soft-toss, giving speech time to real-life Mad Hatters like Howard Dean.

And the Cheshire Cat wonders why *K Street* got put in the Tow Away Zone before the first season was over. Fortunately for America, *K Street* is as close as this cat has gotten to his voice being heard on Capitol Hill. Except when his sci-fi stinker *Solaris* was available in the discount bin at the Blockbuster Video in Georgetown.

Currently, the Cheshire Cat is working on a number of film projects and was recently photographed arriving at the studio in a custom-made hybrid-car that makes a mini-Cooper look like a Hummer. And for this, I applaud him, because, as you know, I'm a longtime conservationist myself. (Although my enlightened conservationism is probably quite different than the "save the maggot" extremism that spews from the Cheshire bin.)

But the absurdity of this maxi-ego exiting this mini-car is worthy of one of the Cheshire's comedies. I remember when these tiny cars would arrive at the circus big top, and an endless stream of clowns would filter out. Well, the clowns are still streaming out. It's just that in Wonderland, they don't know they're clowns.

"It would be so nice if something made sense for a change," says Alice. Yes, honey, it certainly would, but don't expect it out of Wonderland.

Katie Couric
Perki annoyus

KATIE "KoRaN" COURIC

[*Perki annoyus*]

Pygmy Marmosets (PMS) are the smallest and arguably the world's smarmiest monkeys. As such, they have become the favorite pet of morning television talk shows. This particular miniature monkey has for years been trained by its handlers to perform simple tricks in front of the camera, but, limited by its proportionately teeny brain, it can only repeat what it sees other simians doing or saying, thus the phrase, "Monkey see, monkey do." Though considered "cute" by many, the Pygmy Marmoset sports long, fang-like teeth that it flashes when threatened by larger brained mammals, which includes just about all the fauna in the forest and half the flora for that matter.

Perhaps the most profound statement ever made about this performing monkey's television career was by another small, furry creature. Last December in Central Park, a stray dog urinated on an ice sculpture of Couric live on the *Today Show*. Plans are presently being made to build a monument to honor the courageous canine who aptly communicated what the whole of humanity was thinking. I would urge all readers to generously contribute to this worthy cause.

It's really quite difficult to describe exactly what talent Katie Koran, the Pygmy Marmoset, has. This performing primate isn't as stately as Lesley Stahl. She really isn't quite as weepy as Barbara Walters. And she doesn't even have the (relative) gravitas of a Deborah Norville. About as close as PMS has come to actual news reporting are the colonoscopies she subjects America to each year. And I think I speak for the entire nation when I say, "Honey, those emails that say, 'Up yours,' don't really mean it literally." And please, no more on-air breast exams either. You may still be perky, but some of your features are not. Time and gravity catches up with all of us.

What this media monkey really does is mimic what other media monkeys do, but with even less content. In place of pseudo-content, she gives us pseudo-charm so it all kind of works out. For most of us, she's the most annoying thing in the morning since the alarm clock. And unfortunately, no snooze button can make her go away, at least not permanently.

So charmless is PMS in the AM that, by comparison, Matt Lauer is Hugh Grant and Al Roker is Cary. While *Today Show* viewers ask themselves "Where in the World Is Matt Lauer?" I ask myself, "What in the World Is Katie Couric?" and, "Why in the World Does NBC Leave This Living Hangnail on the Air?"

I suppose the role this monkey plays best is that of cheerleader for Team Trotsky, but consider the competition. Eleanor Roosevelt is dead. Jane Fonda's skin is so stretched out, she's afraid to smile, and Barbra Streisand can't memorize the routines. Thirty-some years after getting her certificate of attendance from Dukakis High, our little marmoset remains the perkiest critter on the left side of the sidelines.

Just watch her flirty, flighty method of interviewing. Whether she's chatting with Michael Moore or Idi Amin, our little surrender monkey will look longingly into her guest's eyes, twirl her hair, and giggle like a schoolgirl with a crush. When conducting interviews with Hillary Clinton, I half expect her to ask the senator, between questions about foreign policy, if she thinks Barack Obama is "cute" and if Bill is as "dreamy" at home as he is on camera.

I think she learned her technique at the Torquemada School of Interviewing, Spanish Harlem Branch. Mere seconds after suffering through her piercing, high-pitched chatter, guests will give away anything—trade secrets, fashion tips, bedroom intimacies, Osama bin Laden's home address—*anything*, just to get her to shut up.

But what makes this marmoset especially annoying is her moral preening on issues about which she understands less than zero, less even than George Clooney. And all the while she pretends to be just another soccer mom. Right, and Uday and Qusay's pop was just another soccer dad. PMS's haute-couture haughtiness was best seen when she began complaining to co-host Matt Lauer last summer about gas prices: "It's ridiculous. I had to take out a loan to fill up my minivan. It's crazy."

With her fifteen-million dollar a year salary, she could have been commuting to Pluto and back without worrying about gas prices. In truth, she frets about anything only to the degree she can pin it on Bush, which is just about everything from the temperature of the globe to Sean Penn's two pack a day habit.

Still, NBC's cuddly little monkey has sharp teeth and will bear them when she wants to, as she did in a claw-to-claw scrap with Ann Coulter that the *Washington Post* dubbed "The Morning Mugger versus the Human Uzi." Perhaps what got PMS all hot and bothered for the interview was Coulter's description of her in one of her books as "the affable Eva Braun of morning television" (granted, a gross mischaracterization—I've never found Katie

Koran to be affable). The next thing you know, this seem-ingly mild-mannered marmoset is saying something about "rightwing telebimbo," and the *Today Show* staff starts clearing chairs á la Jerry Springer. It was the best live girl fight on television since Mary McCarthy threw a virtual claw hold on Lillian Hellman twenty-five years ago.

Observe too how the clueless marmoset yearns for the scandal-free days of yore. During the height of the Plamegate investigation last fall, Couric brought in a top presidential ethics expert to discuss President Bush's response—you know, Bill Clinton, the one White House inhabitant who can make Warren Harding look like Abraham Lincoln. But the questions she asked Clinton weren't about his own absurdly scandal-plagued adminis-tration. Instead, she politely asked, "President Bush has said it's a fireable offense now if a crime was committed, but in your view, is the ethical violation enough to warrant dismissal?"

Can you imagine asking Bill Clinton this question? He lowered the nation's unemployment rate by hiring so many independent counsels. If his administration had been held to the same standard PMS holds Bush's, the only ones left in the White House would have been Socks, Buddy, and maybe Chelsea.

It seems this monkey wants to compensate for the softballs she has thrown the Clintons over the years by ball-busting Bush and his cronies. Again, just like a cheerleader, she mindlessly waves her pompoms for her home team (*Bill, Bill, he's our man, if he can't do it, Hillary can!*) and leads the excited lefties in taunts against the righties (*Bush won't help, Bush don't care, Bush has dirty underwear!*).

Now, with her contract set to expire in May of 2006, rumors have circulated that CBS is courting the cute little monkey to fill the seat of Dan "fake but accurate" Rather.

Reportedly, Rather has demanded that his successor be no smarter than he is—a small pool in which even this tiny marmoset can swim with her head proudly above water.

HoWaRD DEAN

This White-Domed Hyena is one of the most unsettling animals in the zoo, a rabid canine that perpetually foams at the mouth and is known for its screeching call that can, strangely enough, only be understood by leaning as far left as possible; those who lean to the right dismiss it as meaningless babble. A pack animal that always travels with its close relative, the braying donkey, this species is particularly afraid of all varieties of elephant. And though the White-Domed Hyena, with its unstable mind and abrasive behavior, is not naturally equipped to take a central role in animal politics, it has in recent years been hastily bred for leadership, resulting in much disorder and confusion in its pack.

Born "Howling" Howard Brush Dean III, 17 November 1948, the son of an art appraiser mother and corporate executive father, the current head of the Democratic National Committee did not set out to become the head of a national party. But, I have to say, I'm glad this dog is the leader of the pack.

Oh, I know what you're thinking. You probably think I feel this way because his mere presence on the political panorama provides so many things to ridicule. Like the way this laughing hyena's neck veins throb whenever he's overly excited—which for this vicious Vermonter is most of the time. The next time you see The Dean Machine launch into one of his frequent, nonsensical rants, just watch—you'll see those veins beating faster than Michael Moore's heart at the sight of an all-you-can-eat buffet.

Also notice that when he speaks at length (which is the only way Blowhoward ever speaks), a caked white substance begins appearing at the corners of his mouth. A physiologist might say that this is dried spittle, caused by nerves, or the foam of a rabid dog. But my bet is that it's the remnants of a lubricant, like Vaseline, that he applies before he speaks so it's easier for him to glide his paw in and out of his mouth without chafing.

I'm also impressed by the hyena's ability to spew so many outrageous, contradictory things. Like when he referred to Republicans as people who "never made an honest living in their lives," and to the G.O.P. as a "white Christian Party." This coming from a white Christian born into a wealthy and prominent New York family that sum-mered in the Hamptons. Highfalutin Howard continued on this path of soft knocks through an exclusive prep school and on to Yale. Although he was eligible for the draft, he received a deferment for an unfused vertebra and spent the next year skiing and bumming around—hitting the slopes, drinking a lot of beer, and dabbling with marijuana. And this privileged poser has the audacity to refer to those who oppose his leftwing lazy-faire philosophies as "white Christians . . . who never made an honest living?"

Well, if that isn't a case of the pothead calling the kettle white!

Of course, as a political commentator, it's hard not to have even a bit of affection for one who provides so much comedic fodder, not the least of which was his defeat speech following the Iowa caucus, where he ended with his now infamous screeching "Yeeeaaahhh!"

That's right, FDR had his "The only thing to fear . . ."

JFK had his "Ask not what your country . . ."

And ADHD had his "Yeeeaaahhh!"

This quickly became known as his "I Have a Scream" speech and immediately placed Howling Howie in the pantheon of laughable lefties.

And what a field day commentators had when, as gover-nor of Vermont, Dean signed the nation's first "civil unions" legislation that allowed same-sex marriages. Almost immedi-ately, the Green Mountain State was filled with high-pitched yodels as joyful Ethans married well-coifed Allens.

But all of the foregoing foolery is merely prelude. The real reason why I like the Dean of Dunces is because this rabid canine actually campaigned for, and was elected, chairman of the Democratic National Committee.

With this Gilligan at the helm, the left-listing Democrat dinghy is sure to capsize, possibly before it even leaves the pier. Initial reports indicate that Dean's seditious statements on Iraq, his snuggling with the estrogen-driven members of Pink Power for Peace, and his overall lack of political acumen have resulted in serious fundraising problems.

Remember, this is a man who has never won any type of political race outside Vermont. A man who had a significant lead in the Iowa caucus and in just two weeks managed to turn that advantage into a distant third-place finish. A man who's as mad as Tom Cruise, Charles Manson, and a hatter combined. And this is the man who the Democrats expect to lead them to victory in 2006.

And that's why it should be no surprise that the White-Domed Hyena is one of my favorite animals in the zoo.

You see, Howling Howie, who really just aspired to be an ordinary party animal but has risen to the top of the food chain, has shown his true spots (as a foaming mad beast) once too often. And, as I'm happy to report, while Dean has garnered much attention—the one thing this hyena has really been scavenging for—this wild animal is leading his unruly pack to utter extinction.

MaUReeN DOWD

[Battleaxea fossilus]

The Capuchin Organ-Grinder Monkey, with its bright shock of red hair and heavily alkaline tongue, is adored by the media elite for playing some of the Left's favorite songs. Though this Paris Hilton of prose can only play simple tunes, like *Old Man Rumsfeld Had a War*, and tired refrains such as "Georgie Porgie, puddin' and pie, stole the election and made us cry," the repetitive motion of the editorial grinder keeps the monkey in a perpetual frenzy of ecstatic song and dance. This crafty monkey must be watched carefully, though, as during its performance, it is prone to pick the pockets of unsuspecting onlookers and purposely fabricate or misquote the statements of higher species. Of all animals in the zoo, the Capuchin Monkey has the most difficult time finding a mate, not because of an advanced intelligence, as the monkey often contends, but for the simple fact that this creature is thoroughly unlikable.

I hope Maureen Dowd doesn't read her reviews. They're not good. *Wall Street Journal* columnist Peggy Noonan says, "Maureen Dowd has mined new depths of shallowness." And Myrna Blyth comments, "Whenever I see Maureen on TV, that wonderful old English phrase 'Mutton dressed as lamb' pops into my mind." Even that ancient mariner Melvin Lasky in his book, *The Language of Journalism*, goes so far as to call her "a jejune commentator, confined to immature language and a teenage superciliousness, trying to cope mewlishly with some of the most complex and melancholy affairs of state." OK, I admit, I had to look "jejune" up too. It means "lacking maturity." Works for me.

The hot-flashing, red-headed editorial grinder for the Gray Lady has taken some sharp hits from her fellow journalists, liberal and conservative alike, for her alkaline style and her over-imaginative journalism. When she's not short on facts, she's twisting them or simply ignoring them to make her case.

In her bi-weekly op-ed column, the Capuchin Monkey plays the same old tunes about those mean old Bushies and congressional Republicans with the only variations being the erratic wanderings we have come to expect from a simian-American tunesmith.

In a world of what seems like increasingly debased standards, this sneering simian won a Pulitzer Prize. But then again, so did the *Times'* Walter Duranty. He won his for concealing Stalin's seven-million death terror-famine. This little game of hide-the-holocaust secured FDR's recognition of the Soviet Union and a front row seat for Duranty at the recognition ceremony. Pulitzer standards may not have changed that much after all. Almost as amusing, this monkey won her Pulitzer for "distinguished commentary," just beating out Jerry Springer's "Final Thought" and David Letterman's "Top Ten" list.

This all just goes to prove the theory that if you let a monkey bang away at a typewriter twice a week for ten years, it will eventually write a Maureen Dowd column. During her tenure at the *Times*, Dowd's writing has gone from only half bad to egregious. Duranty has not been her only role model. There's also Jayson Blair, who put cows in Jessica Lynch's front yard and got fired for it, and Herbert Matthews, who put the "anti-communist" Fidel Castro in power and got promoted. "I got my job through *The New York Times*," read the dead-on caption beneath a *National Review* caricature of the Left's favorite cigar-smoking mass murderer—in this hemisphere at least. This was also a lesson learned for Dowd: Big lies work much better than little ones.

In May 2003, Dowd got caught in a little monkey busi-ness of her own. To be specific, she quoted President Bush in her column as saying the following about Al

Qaeda: "That group of terrorists who attacked our country is slowly but surely being decimated... They're not a problem anymore."

Here is what Bush actually said as she well knew, "That group of terrorists who attacked our country is slowly, but surely being decimated. Right now, about half of all the top Al Qaeda operatives are either jailed or dead. In either case, they're not a problem anymore."

In other words, she had doctored a quote by President Bush to make it sound as if W were dismissing the threat by "Al Qaeda terrorists." Of course, the actual White House transcript showed Bush saying that *dead and captured* Al Qaeda terrorists were no longer a threat. All the news that fits, she prints, and those few extra words must have exceeded her limit.

Within hours, however, a whole flock of media sheep were passing off Dowd's subversion as conventional wisdom, and hundreds of papers ran it in her nationally fabricated column. When the falsification was revealed, the *Old York Times* made no attempt to correct its star editorialist, this Lorena Bobbitt of the printed word. Knowing the *Times*, its editors likely submitted her butchered column for a Pulitzer. At least she didn't steal it from someone in San Antonio. At least there is a George W. Bush. True, news outlets like the *News Tribune* of Tacoma, Washington, and the *Lufkin (Texas) Daily News* printed red-faced retractions, but the *Times* didn't feel the need. It doesn't make mistakes.

Understandable, I suppose. For if the *Times* had to write a retraction every time they printed a false statement, they would have to hire an all-new staff, dozens of prolific writers, all working around the clock, like Santa's elves, just to keep up with the workload. Heck, they could plug in a retraction supplement for each issue right after the classifieds. It could replace the funnies.

A few weeks after the shameful misquote, the Capuchin Monkey—like a thief returning to the scene of her crime—used the Bush quote again in a column, this time undoctored, but without even mentioning her earlier cut-and-paste job. Because of this whole affair, a new word crept into the journalistic vocabulary: "Dowdify."

After repeated gaffes by the *New York Times'* editorialists and incessant catcalls from their less obsequious journalistic peers, the paper was forced to announce in October 2005 that the editorial page writers would finally be held to the same lame journalistic standards as the rest of the staff. They could continue to say any fool thing they wanted, but now the Times would run a retraction—in *Times'* fashion, where no one could see it. It took the editors two years after the malicious Bush misquote to do just this.

And what prompted the change? Dowd and two of her

colleagues repeated the same error in each of their respective columns. Would that be called re-dowdification? Or just plain stupid?

At least it's nice to see that there is a rock-bottom standard below which the *Times* won't sink—for now at least. But the Capuchin Monkey's editors can't guarantee that she still won't try. Just look at her backstab of fellow *Times* reporter Judith Miller, whom she accused of destroying the paper's credibility—as if! Miller protected her White House source and went to prison for it, for which Dowd called her a "Woman of Mass Destruction." That's a pun. Dowd is reputed to be a humorist.

Recently, our performing simian has taken a break from grinding out her column to hawk her most current book, *Are Men Necessary?* The book really should have been titled, *Sexless in the City* or *Why Am I Not Married in My Mid-Fifties?* That's the topic Dowd really obsesses about. The reason she offers for her tiresome single status is that her intelligence and professional accomplishments frighten men away.

Sure, Dowdy, you keep telling yourself that. But the fact is that, as you dance around the *Old York Times* like a performing monkey, the handful of red-blooded males in your metrosexual part of the jungle can smell an organ grinder from a hundred yards away. And they don't want you anywhere near theirs.

DIANNE FeiNSTeiN

[*Mao zedongus*]

The Frisco Red Heron is a standout bird known for its heroic migration: the famed "Long Flight" from the Bay Area to the Chinese homeland during the annual August congressional recess to meet up with its mate. In China, it is known as the "Hidden Dragon" Heron and is kept as a pet by many higher-up Chinese Communist Party officials. The Red Heron is particularly possessive about its privacy and property (and can regularly be spotted clucking for its collectivist causes), though it readily invades all other birds' habitats as it feels necessity warrants.

137

Gulfstream liberals have their own congressional caucus headed by one of their own, Senator Dianne Feinstein of California. As one of the wealthiest birds in this well appointed aviary, the Red Heron sits on her gilded political perch preaching to the lowly, unwashed masses of American mammals, promising to make our meager and meaningless lives better and safer. And aren't we all grateful?

The Red Heron's policies are, not surprisingly, socialist, marked by odd occasional moments of lucidity. When she isn't playing useful idiot for her husband's Chinese government partners, she still closely follows the Democratic Party flock, breaking with them on the rarest of moments when reason, logic, and pure political self-interest crash down on her like a rickety building in a 9.0 earthquake.

The Red Heron can appear at time to be hawkish, and sometimes patriotic, like her performance immediately after 9/11. However, she can easily turn dove, but never a lonesome one, as she is a creature of the flock and will fly wherever the prevailing wind and its flighty ideology take it.

Similarly, she can boldly champion her fascist principles, and then turn around and make believe she never said any such thing. It's not easy being a useful idiot. It takes discipline, balance, and the brain of a bird.

One additional role that she plays is stool pigeon. According to a 1997 investigation by the *Los Angeles*

Times, Feinstein was pushing the Clinton administration for dropping trade restrictions on China at exactly the same time that her husband was increasing his financial investment there. They assured everyone that there was a strict "firewall" between her foreign policy positions and his equity positions in China. But this "firewall" is not the Great Wall of China, seeing as how Dick Blum has repeatedly traveled with Feinstein to China, and her prestige as a U.S. senator has opened many doors for her husband to the highest levels of the Communist Chinese government. Since Feinstein entered the Senate, Blum's China portfolio has grown from $500,000 to $2 to 3 billion today. What a coincidence. Maybe he took Hillary's class in cattle futures trading.

Just how many American lawmakers and their foreign investment banker spouses do you think have slept in Mao's old bed at the invitation of the Chinese president? And we thought that Democrats were just selling out in the Lincoln Bedroom. Who knew that, once again, the Clintons were just imitating China?

The Red Heron took the side of the Chinese in 2001 when one of their fighter pilots intentionally collided with one of our unarmed surveillance planes over international waters. She told CNN, "I want the Chinese to know that I, as senior senator from California, am deeply sorry about the loss of a Chinese pilot," squeaking out a tearful apology and saying, "We're sorry," all while the Bush administration was trying to negotiate the release of the American flight crew.

But even though the Red Heron has to deal with her socialist schizophrenia, it behooves me to admit that she's the more sensible of the two California senators. And by sensible, I mean she doesn't spit on you when she squawks—or foam at the mouth, like the California Cackle Hen.

As witness to the Red Heron's authoritarian voting record, consider that as one of the more liberal senators in Congress, she consistently has one of the worst ACLU legislative ratings among Democrats for things like free speech, personal privacy, and government powers. How it must break the heart of the ACLU, of all organizations, to clip the wings of a Democrat, and a liberal one at that. They don't mind so much beating up on the yellow dogs, but the Red Herons are another issue.

Needless to say, the Red Heron works hard to destroy your liberties. One of her main causes has been the establishment of a National ID. She even sponsored a bill to mandate one. In order to make this work, the Red Heron and her birds of like feather would tie it to our Social Security numbers. And as anyone that has caught even one local newscast over the past ten years realizes, one of the fastest growing crimes in America is identity theft. And just how do they steal your identity? One answer: your

Social Security number. Once someone gets hold of that, you're pretty much who they want you to be. And why does this one little piece of information put you into so much jeopardy? Because nitwits in Congress have for years expanded the use of Social Security numbers to tighten the noose on personal liberties and allow nosy federalistas to keep tabs on you.

As an elected official from California, doesn't the Red Heron realize that it is less risky for illegal immigrants to purchase a Social Security number than to smoke cigarettes indoors?

But don't think for a minute that Feinstein isn't conflicted on this issue. She once complained that it took her less than three minutes on the Internet to find her Social Security number online. She then was able in a couple of clicks to locate a map to her house for the wacko who wanted to deliver her a pipe bomb pizza. Suddenly, she's the privacy queen. However, don't be fooled in thinking that she's given up on tagging and branding and iris scanning every American citizen. If she has her way, the most commonly heard phrase in America will morph from "Do you want fries with that?" to "Papers please."

This Red Heron is also notoriously anti-Second Amendment. In 1995, she famously declared on *60 Minutes* about her attempts to ban firearm ownership: "If I could have gotten fifty-one votes in the Senate of the United States for an outright ban, picking up every one of them,

Mr. and Mrs. America, turn 'em all in, I would have done it." Well, at least she's honest about her intent. If it works in China, why not here?

First off, hasn't Feinstein heard of this thing called the Constitution, and the section within called the Second Amendment? The Constitution isn't like an elevator that skips the thirteenth floor. Every one of the amendments matter.

Isn't it instructive how certain senators choke when a judicial nominee mentions anything about the "original intent," but when it comes to the Second Amendment, they are suddenly fluent on colonial militias and the War for Independence? If only they actually cared about original intent. One has to read deep into that famed penumbra to figure out why some senators want to define federally-licensed gun dealers as "street gangs" to more easily prosecute them for illegal sales. Fortunately, this bill has not gone too far beyond our bird's brain.

One other curiosity: Whenever the Red Heron speaks about gun control, she skips over the fact that she herself has a concealed carry permit and likes to pack heat. If the California Cackle Hen merely hires armed guards, the Red Heron is a regular pistol-packing mama. Thank God she spares us helots from the danger and responsibility of carrying a gun. How could we ever manage?

Speaking of the Constitution, perhaps one of the most insidious institutions in American government is the judicial politburo that she and the California Cackle Hen have established in the Ninth Circuit Court. Threatening to blue-slip (Senate legalese for blackball) every Bush judicial nomination for California, these two coerced Attorney General Gonzalez into setting up four bipartisan commissions to select federal judges for California circuit courts. Three members of each commission are selected by Bush, and three others are selected by the hen and the heron. Four members are needed to prevent these birds of a judicial feather from blackballing a candidate. No other state delegation in the Senate has such a set-up. And where in the Constitution do our elected chicks find authorization for their own hand-picked apparatchiks? It's apparently in the "living" part.

That's not even the half of it. Given the Red Heron's attempts to ban alcohol on all U.S. airlines, to force federal officials to purchase guns from her preferred foreign suppliers (Chinese, as you might expect), to publicly call the U.S. "an environmental slacker" while driving around in one of her five SUVs, or to oppose judicial nominees because they're too serious about a religious faith other than Wiccan, we ought to be lucky that the Red Heron and her left-winged friends have left us with any freedoms at all.

After all, who needs constitutional niceties? The fleeced "flock" is a much better paradigm for a Democrat's ideal America.

Newt Gingrich
Spinelus cavinien

NEWT GING RICH

The Georgia GOPAC Tick is a hard-shelled but soft-headed pest that sustains itself by sucking the blood out of any organism that will increase the tick's much-desired power drive. It gains natural advantages through its seeming intelligence and clever concealment of weaknesses. While the GOPAC Tick aggressively latches onto any available host it can find, including prospective mates, it quickly retreats at the sight of organized resistance or the onset of illness. Promised a "Contract for America"; instead gave us a "Contract on America." Like a Trojan Horse, the GOPAC Tick can change colors with the landscape, and recently struck a deal with the Limber Leopard, seeing she will likely be the next power on the throne. Several sightings of this rare tick have been reported recently in both Iowa and New Hampshire perennial breeding grounds for pests of all sorts. This tick is also known to spread numerous diseases including *Severe Disappointeria* and *Acute Apathyosis*.

145

The story of Newt "the GOPAC Tick" Gingrich is a sad one. It's a story of shattered dreams and broken promises. The story of how one visionary little crawler fed off the hot blood of outrage and enthusiasm, sucking all it could from the discontent of the American Eagle. It rode this host all the way from the tick's home state of Georgia to the hallowed halls of Congress. So engorged did the tick become, however, on the ingested fluids of his power base, that he finally popped and splattered all over the Eagle's right wing while its left wing kept right on flapping.

It's the story of How the Gingrich Stole Christmas.

It's hard to deny that the Republican Revolution of 1994 was spawned by the tick's limited vision. And it was a brilliant and noble idea, begun with the best of intentions. But as we all know, the road to Hell—like the road to its sister city, Washington—is paved with good intentions.

Gingrich boldly committed the great bulk of the Republican Party—most every member of both the House and the Senate by extension—to the Contract with America: a revolutionary commitment in writing, describing plans to shrink the size of government, limit the U.N.'s role in American foreign policy, lower taxes, and implement significant welfare reform, among other things. The Contract was laid out in precise detail.

So far, so good. But so what? Even the most casual camper knows that you never enter a contract with a pest.

There is no such thing as a beneficial tick. The crawler fattens itself on your precious bodily fluids, and what do you get in return? Sucked dry. And maybe sick for good measure.

So it was with Gingrich.

Once the Republicans were in power, things went well for a while. Bills were passed, taxes cut. His colleagues named Gingrich Speaker of the House. *Time* magazine named him "Tick of the Year." The blood he was sucking, alas, started swelling his head.

By 1995, when the GOPAC Tick and his colleagues drew up their seven-year balanced budget plan, he was too swollen to maneuver, too swell-headed to chance his newfound prestige. The president swatted down the proposed budget—historically important as the first time Clinton said "no" to anything—and the Republican Congress quickly found itself without a serious strategy to sting back.

When the government shut down for lack of funding, the media poured all its dread daily thumping (DDT) on the GOPAC Tick and his vacillating band. What? He didn't expect this? He hadn't immunized himself and his colleagues to a media spray in advance? No, the tick's strategy in the face of DDT was what the French, who have more words for "surrender" than Eskimos do for snow, call "sauve qui peut," or—in American—"run for your lives, every tick for itself." And so the revolution ended, not with a bang from a real bug's bug, but a whimper from a wimp's wimp.

They say Henry Clay was "The Great Compromiser." But that was long before Gingrich, the tick who, upon encountering real resistance, caved in faster than a punctured lung. The GOPAC Tick, we found out, is the kind of eager parasite that could have struck a deal with Pol Pot: *"Very well. You can beat us, shackle us, and make us dig our own graves. Just as we long as we get to stay in your fine capital city. That's our final offer."*

In less time than it takes George W. Bush to read an issue of *Ranger Rick*, the Republican Revolution of 1994 withered into history, leaving about as much lasting impression as the Disco Revolution of 1974.

Once the Republicans faltered, public confidence waned, and with the impeachment procedures that followed, GOPAC's once loyal constituents grew weary of the flea circus. Democrats actually gained seats from the Republicans in the impeach-or-not-to-impeach '98 election.

All of these maneuvers merely revealed the true colors of this blood-hungry biter, an insect whose principles proved as soft and swollen as his gut. Even in the early days of his congressional career, the tick's character was suspect. He was rumored to prey on his female staff members. Those rumors grew when this insect, apparently not wanting to suck any chemo with the blood, divorced his first wife while she was recovering from cancer.

Lovely, Gingrich. Why don't you pay a visit to the local orphanage and kick some kids in the shins while you're at it?

The same deranged scenario repeated itself immediately after Gingrich stepped down as Speaker and left the House. He announced his divorce to his second wife right after she'd been diagnosed with MS. He left her for a congressional aide twenty-three years his junior.

Even in his love life, the GOPAC Tick is dangerous, bleeding his partner to the point of disease, then moving on to another host. Forget *Time's* "Tick of the Year." The man deserves the "Woody Allen Award" for his cold dexterity in betraying and preying.

The irony, of course, is that all this was going on while the tick's colleagues hammered away at Clinton's moral failures and pushed impeachment. And they wondered why the GOPAC Tick just buzzed awkwardly in the background.

Now, I know full well that only he who is without sin should swat that first pest. Don't get me wrong here. I don't want to smash this tick to extinction. I just want him to shut up and go away. But he won't. He keeps turning up, looking for fresh blood.

Although Gingrich is a private tick again, he has been nearly as pesky as Jimmy Carter—no, forgive me, not quite *that* pesky. No one is that pesky. (What is it about Georgia?) While Gingrich rightly criticized the State

Department in a recent speech, saying that bureaucrats there were undercutting the president's foreign policy, his attack had been coordinated and approved by Bush administration officials beforehand. There's that pesky GOPAC Tick again, doing the White House's dirty work.

Any White House's! That's the rub. This tick doesn't want to fly on his own power. He wants to fly in Air Force One. Recently, he aligned himself with Hillary Clinton on healthcare and national security issues, effectively moderating the credentials of a woman he once painted to the left of Mao. She hasn't changed, Gingrich. It's you, bro!

Which reminds me—you know how every time you come in from the woods, you check for ticks. That's what I do every time I come back from Washington. I check for Newt.

You just never know who he'll latch onto next.

Ruth Bader Ginsburg
Litigatus agitatus

RuTH "GATOR" GiNSBuRG

[Litigatus agitatus]

The Bader Gator, a dangerous breed of the combative Liti-Gator family, is notorious for clamping down on its Constitution prey and dragging it below the water in a death roll to drown out our freedoms and to feast on them at a later time where no can see. Native to the legal swamps of New York, this unseemly creature is easily the most aggressively progressive animal on the political zoo's Kangaroo Court and regularly tries to subvert the zoo's rules. Strangely, the Bader Gator seems to long even for the brutal controls of foreign zoos and circuses, where animals, particularly elephants, are regularly abused. The Bader Gator is known to have an extraordinarily long life span.

When Bill Clinton nominated Ruth "Gator" Ginsburg to replace Byron White as associate justice of the Supreme Court in 1993, there was very little protest by Senate Republicans, despite the fact that they were about to confirm one of America's most radical attorneys to the highest court of the land. In fact, she breezed through the confirmation process and, in less than six weeks, was approved 96-3.

Even at that time, her extremist views were well known. The Bader Gator had served as the chief litigator for the Women's Rights Project of the ACLU, and served on their national board of directors. During her tenure, this board called for the repealing of laws against child pornography and decriminalization of adult/child sex. If NAMBLA had a pin-up girl, an oxymoronic concept I admit, the Bader Gator would probably be it. It's a horrible image, regardless.

Even more directly, the Bader Gator had coauthored a paper for the U.S. Commission on Civil Rights that called for, among other things, the legalization of prostitution and bigamy, as well as lowering the age of consent for sex down to twelve. She also said that groups like the Boy Scouts and Girl Scouts should be banned from receiving any kind of public support because they "perpetuated stereotyped sex roles." (Of course, it makes sense that this gator would be opposed to such stereotypes as she has all the femininity and sensuality of a cactus.)

Now you would think that all of this controversy would

have gotten at least some Republican senators aroused enough to pull out the pitchforks and make some hay, but it didn't. Those were the days when Trent "King Coif" Lott was more concerned about the state of his hair than the state of the nation, and his Republican colleagues were no more animated.

During her confirmation hearings, the Bader Gator refused to answer specific questions about how she would approach certain issues, thereby establishing the now famous "Ginsburg Precedent." Post-Gator Supreme Court nominees can now swim unimpeded through their hearings without telling America, let alone the Senate, what kind of justices they would make during their lifetime appointments.

But even this stonewalling didn't prevent the Bader Gator from letting her judicial philosophy be made known. Earlier in her career, she had applauded instances when the Supreme Court had "creatively interpreted clauses of the Constitution to accommodate a modern vision" of jurisprudence. That means she was glad when they made stuff up as long as that stuff fit with her wobbly worldview. At the hearing, the Bader Gator also let slip her belief that judges could serve as "interim legislatures" when the legislatures didn't act how she wanted them to, which, in her book, was just about always. Ah, democracy and the constitutional separation of powers are sissy stuff!

At least with the Phantom, David Souter, Republicans

could claim that they were bamboozled into thinking he would honor the Constitution. With the Bader Gator, they didn't have any such excuse. They knew from the get-go that she didn't give a flip about the Constitution, the Bill of Rights, or the Declaration, let alone the opinion page of the *Wall Street Journal*. Still, the clueless conservatives approved her overwhelmingly for the High Court.

In the thirteen years that she's been on the court, the Bader Gator has amazingly become even more radical, if you can believe that's possible. And the consequences of her radicalism would make James Madison do half-gainers in his grave.

Let's see now, Texas gays have a constitutional right to commit sodomy, and Nebraska docs have a constitutional right to kill babies as they are coming out of the womb—which amendment was that now?—but once out, that child can do anything he or she pleases for the next eighteen years since the state has no right to convict young folks of a capital crime, no matter how heinous. In fact, the Bader Gator believed that no state had any right to make any law until *Gore v. Bush*, in which the state laws of Florida, at least as interpreted by its twisted judiciary, became suddenly sacrosanct.

Oh, yea, and states do have the right to take your property even if just to hand it over to some other, presumably better connected, property owner (should we be surprised that the ACLU doesn't include rulings on property rights when they rate Supreme Court justices?). At least when Attilla burned your house down he did not try to convince you he was advancing the public good by increasing the tax base. The gator's Constitution lives uniquely in Ruth Gator Ginsburg's reptilian mind.

Her latest leftist *cause de jour* is trying to convince her court colleagues that the restrictive nature of our "outdated" Constitution requires them to look to the laws of other "enlightened" countries for inspiration and direction. "Judges in the United States are free to consult all manner of commentary," she said in a speech last year.

In other words, she would rather judges rely on what courts in Canada, France, and the Netherlands are doing to advance neo-Trotskyism than to abide by the will of the people who are paying her salary as reflected in the Constitution.

The net effect is that the Constitution becomes a "living" document to be interpreted as our lifetime philosopher-kings see fit (what she calls a "boldly dynamic interpretation departing radically from the original understanding"). And worse, it becomes irrelevant altogether if some foreign judge is advancing some more attractive perversion. This is the judicial legacy we have received from both of Clinton's Supreme Court nominees—the Bader Gator and Stephen Breyer. To be sure, the ACLU types went berserk over *Gore v. Bush*, that was much too much of a "living" decision even for them.

One area of jurisprudence where she has combined the "legal wisdom" of other countries with her idea of a "living" Constitution concerns the death penalty. Never mind that the Constitution explicitly permits capital punishment for crimes like treason; no, imposing the ultimate penalty is considered "cruel and unusual punishment" in this internationalist's mind, and therefore unconstitutional.

In 2002, she convinced enough of her Court colleagues to prohibit the death penalty on the mentally retarded. The killer in this case had an IQ of 59 but still knew enough about what he was doing to kill his victim in a remote field. And when questioned by the police, he blamed the murder on his buddy. He knew what he was doing was wrong. So just as the Bader Gator invented the "Ginsburg Precedent" for judicial nominees, she has now invented the "Ginsburg Defense," where instead of claiming insanity, defendants can now claim to be an idiot. How appropriate.

And Ginsburg's recent advice to juvenile killers? Kill at will, at least until you're eighteen, because thanks to the Bader Gator and her pack of reptiles, murderers convicted before they are adults can't be put to death. Should parents now be more afraid of their children, or was this a way for Ginsburg to inadvertently help criminals use children as assassins?

But the Constitution isn't the only thing that the Bader Gator wants to put in a death roll. Now she is eyeing Supreme Court traditions as well. In an uncharacteristic campaign gesture for a sitting Supreme Court Justice, the Bader Gator snapped publicly that "not any woman will do" to replace Justice O'Connor because there are "some women who might be appointed who would not advance human rights or women's rights." Yo, Gator, judges aren't supposed to "advance" anything. They're supposed to "follow" the law.

Now here's the arrogance of the Bader Gator's position writ large: How could she anticipate that the best person for the job would have been a female? And do you think that when she talked about human and women's rights, she had in mind the view held by most Federalist Society members, or the over imaginative views held by her fellow reptiles at the ACLU?

This is how reptilian the leftist judicial thinking has become. At least the Bader Gator is clear about her intentions to force her radical agenda down the throats of America, whether the citizens like it or not. But heaven help us if a case ever comes up before the Court considering a prohibition of sodomizing Boy Scouts. She might vote to overturn that law on the precedent that it discriminates against those with a weakness for children.

She has an awfully big mouth, and a big bun for a tail. It won't be easy, but maybe Jungle Sam Alito can finally wrestle this Bader Gator into submission.

Rudy Giuliani
Newyorkus pseudo-conservatus

RuDY GIULIANI

[*Newyorkus pseudo-conservatus*]

The Gotham Gazelle moves effortlessly across the plains of Central Park and uses its speed and agility to elude all political predators. Best suited to terrains east of the Hudson, the Gotham Gazelle has been spotted in recent months as far away as New Hampshire or even Iowa, its unruly mane cut back to fighting trim. An animal known to have an ill temper and a propensity to not run with its own pack, the Gotham Gazelle feeds on headlines and generous self-promotion.

Sometimes a man defines a moment; at other times, a moment will define the man. But few would deny that both were true for Rudy Giuliani on 9/11. Ever since that great and terrible day when extraordinary heroism became an ordinary and, in many cases, a still unsung virtue, the Gotham Gazelle gracefully and forcefully embodied the spirit of resolve of the American people to stand up to the predatory pack of Islamofascists.

Just think for a moment about what this gazelle had to face when he got up that fateful morning. He had a professional reputation as an unyielding hothead, a personal resumé that bordered on the scandalous, more political enemies than Kim Jong-Il, and a political philosophy that was half Rockefeller, half Dirty Harry.

The mayoral primary that day was to be a sign of the end of his reign over New York City. He had no real political prospects in the future, having squandered his golden opportunity against Hillary in 2000. All the while, the disintegration of his second marriage and the details of his affair with another woman were being chronicled on the gossip pages of New York's dailies, which had forced him out of Gracie Mansion, now the home of his wife and children. Giuliani was forced to sleep in the spare bedroom in a friend's place (a gay couple's home, by the way), not the natural habitat for a gazelle. His stock was in an Enron-like dive on the morning of 9/11.

But by the end of the day, his sins had been forgiven by the people of New York City, and all of America for that matter. And his image as a public figure had been completely recast with the entire world watching.

For all his many faults, the one thing he gave his city and the country that day was leadership. And it had absolutely nothing to do with politics. He was a gazelle on a mission, who sprinted to the head of the fold. With the rest of our country's politicians scrambling for cover, his was the only image that America saw that day. What we saw was gravity and determination, realism and optimism. And America needed it.

Think for a minute about who could have been the face of New York on 9/11. It could have been Hillary standing there with that blank look on her face framed by that stupid little Yankees hat competing for camera time with her chubby hubby. It could have been Chuck Schumer, who, when not trying to hide under a rock, would have been fighting Hillary for a place in the lens. "I don't care if that tower is collapsing, get that camera over here!" Or it could have been Charlie Rangel or Al Sharpton, there to tell us how America was being punished for its racism and support of Israel, all the while demanding contracts for the diversity training needed to mend those rifts. Or even worse, it could have been Hudson Hippo Jerry Nadler, the Democratic congressman for lower

Manhattan, whose appearance would have only given the terrorists further encouragement to strike again. With anyone from this cast of characters representing America on September 11th, who would have blamed the terrorists for launching another attack?

Thankfully, Giuliani was the man. By sheer personality, he pushed Pataki to the background. Although as tall as Osama, Governor George lacks Bin Laden's charm and ease before the camera. Indeed, on a bad day, he could make Al Gore look like Jay Leno.

No, the task was left to the Gotham Gazelle to leap forward and help lead America through that dark day. He understood that it wasn't a day for political posturing or settling political scores. And in the end, it wasn't about him. It was about the thousands of innocent victims that were taken from their families in New York, Pennsylvania, and the Pentagon. It was about the dozens of friends he lost that day who made up the bulk of the city's leadership. And it was about the hundreds of police and firemen who gave their lives to remind a long-wandering America that there are values worth fighting and dying for. And in the days and months that followed, that was the legacy that the Gotham Gazelle strove valiantly to preserve.

The man made the moment, and the moment made the man.

You have to wonder where the gazelle goes from here. He cannot win west of the Hudson for numerous reasons. Mainly because of his liberalism and his experience during and after 9/11 which was so transforming that it would be difficult to translate his popularity back into politics without diminishing it. You see, not every day is September 11. Most days are like September 10. A president gets up, has breakfast, passes bills, signs executive orders, appoints judges, chooses cabinet members. And every day the Gotham Gazelle spends in the White House is another day we would be holding our breath. The last six years have been hard enough. After four years, Giuliani could turn the whole country blue—in every sense of the word.

Maybe in New York City, you have to suck up to gays and baby killers and racial hucksters to stay in office, but that kind of sucking up can be habit forming.

To change metaphors for a moment, we are the frog to Giuliani's scorpion. He asks us for a ride across the river. We say, "But if we go near you, you'll sting us and kill us." He says, "But if I sting you, we'll both drown. Why would I do that?"

"Good point," we say and offer the scorpion a ride on our back. Sure enough, half way across, the scorpion stings us. We start to drown and take him with us. "Why did you do that?" we ask with our dying breath.

Says the scorpion, "It's in my nature."

The one time he tried to act like a conservative, when he threatened to withhold funding for an art museum featuring a portrait of the Virgin Mary in elephant dung, as soon as his liberal friends piped up in opposition, he remembered his truer nature and quickly backed down.

So let us keep Giuliani in our memory as a gazelle and not a scorpion. Better to remember him as the guy who saved New York rather than the guy who lost New Hampshire. To throw his hat back into the ring would open up a lot of personal questions this gazelle doesn't want chasing after him, much like we saw during the Bernie Kerik scandal that burst open after Rudy pushed for his former consulting partner's nomination to head the Department of Homeland Security. It would also mean that he would have to defend himself from people in his own party who now idolize him but who would have to take issue with his barely-Republican policies.

What conservative wouldn't have grave reservations for a man who has said publicly that he would give his daughter money for an abortion, and thinks that the government should raid your wallet for the cause as well? And Rudy would be just as likely to host mass gay weddings in the East Room of the White House as Hillary would. Nor would he be above turning the Lincoln Bedroom into a love nest for Bernie Kerik (hey, if Bill

Clinton can do it). How many conservatives are going to line up their support behind that platform?

No, just like a prizefighter that fights beyond his prime, the best thing the Gotham Gazelle could do is to hang up his hooves and rest content at having had his moment and transformed it.

In a zoo—and there is no more zoo of a zoo than Washington—gazelles lose their charm more quickly than any other animal. To see them at their best, you have to see them in action, in their natural habitat—in the Gotham Gazelle's case, the streets of New York, predators be damned.

AL Gore

Pumice ignoramus

AL GORE

[*Pumice ignoramus*]

The *Pumice ignoramus*, the most ignorant of the igneous family of rock, is a form of lava with gas bubbles in it. At the Savage Menagerie, this stone-faced lump, having no personality or character to speak of, is kept as a Pet Rock and lacks the sensibility of even the most primitive of animals therein. One would ignore the Pet Rock altogether if its gas bubbles did not occasionally rise to the surface and leave a remarkably unpleasant stench. Because of this progressive's lack of forward progress, the Pet Rock will on occasion develop a thick swath of moss which has often been mistaken for a beard.

What more can be said about Al Gore, the Democrats' Pet Rock? So dense is this blockhead that he lost several debates to W, about whom he recently said, "I think he is plenty smart." By comparison to you, Rocky, yes, W is Immanuel Kant.

Had I ventured to catalogue Rocky's many adventures in denseness—his invention of the Internet, his claim to be the Oliver of *Love Story*, his sit-down with the Buddhist nuns, his phony "dying breath" speech at the 1996 convention—I would have had no room for any of the other creatures in my zoo. In fact, I was just about to give Rocky a pass for irrelevance when those gas bubbles rose to the surface once again, and they did so in that bastion of free speech and civil behavior, Saudi Arabia.

Those who have followed Rocky's career were not surprised. As we all know, Rocky turned bitter when he realized that his fellow Dems had underestimated the votes they would have to steal to win the election of 2000. Where was Richard Daley when he needed him? Not the Bozo son they sent to Florida, but the real one, the guy who put JFK in the White House.

In a speech to the MoveOn.orgy crowd just before the first transfer of power to the Iraqi people, Rocky welcomed this new democracy by describing the liberation of Iraq as part of the Bush plan for global dominance. Rocky claimed publicly that it was "as repugnant to the rest of the world as the ugly dominance of the helpless, naked Iraqi prisoners has been to the American people."

While he was at it, Rocky also accused his president of having "launched an unprecedented assault on civil liberties." Now remember, this is coming from a guy whose White House began its tenure with a tank and gas attack against a religious community that killed eighty, including twenty children, and ended with a jackbooted kidnapping of a six-year-old boy and his quick dispatch to the worker's paradise of Cuba.

Rocky climaxed this talk by claiming that Bush "brought deep dishonor to our country and built a durable reputation as the most dishonest president since Richard Nixon." No, Rocky, compared to your boss, the impeached perjurer you gallantly defended as "one of our greatest presidents," Nixon is Honest Abe, and Bush is Mother Teresa.

If I wasn't prepared to forgive Rocky his denseness, I was at least prepared to forget. That was until he went to the Jiddah Economic Forum in early 2006. If you remember, the Saudi royalty, including the Bin Laden family, staged this event. These are the same people who are exporting Wahabbi madmen all over the world, the same people who stonewalled us on the Khobar Towers bombing, the same people who volunteered fifteen of their most deranged sons for their day of aviation glory on September 11.

There, in this hellhole of a country, at the height of the

worldwide cartoon jihad, Rocky had the nerve to attack the Bush administration for its "terrible abuses" of Arabs since September 11. As to specifics, he claimed that Arabs had been "indiscriminately rounded up, often on minor charges of overstaying a visa or not having a green card in proper order, and held in conditions that were just unforgivable." Hey, Rocky, Americans in Saudi Arabia have suffered much worse for drinking a Bud at a backyard barbecue, and I'm not remotely joking. At least we didn't behead anyone.

Let us not forget too that in the run-up to the 9/11 hearings, Rocky and his fellow Dems were lambasting the president for not being vigilant enough.

"Unfortunately there have been terrible abuses and it's wrong," said this pathological suck-up to his decadent hosts. "I do want you to know that it does not represent the desires or wishes or feelings of the majority of the citizens of my country."

No, you ignominious piece of igneous, that roundup of Arab lawbreakers did absolutely represent the will of the American people, which is why, happily, there will be no rose garden in your future, just a rock garden.

For as with all Pet Rocks, Al Gore works best when he just sits there like a lump—doing and saying nothing, just sweating in the sun.

Jesse Jackson

Extortus exploitus

JeSSe JaCKSoN

[Extortus exploitus]

The Reverend Vulture is a well-heeled, well-dressed scavenger in sheep's clothing that feeds off the death and decay in the political jungle. Observing the cycle of life from a pious perch, the Reverend Vulture does all its praying with an "e." It swoops down and begins feasting on any creature showing signs of distress, be they live or dead, including animals from its own flock. Its lightness of conscience and lack of gravity give the Reverend Vulture the speed and dexterity to beat all other scavengers to just about any cultural rot that has attracted a camera crew. And just as kings and queens of yore used trained falcons, so do today's petty potentates and two bit tyrants use the Reverend Vulture.

Only in an environment without real predators can a jive turkey like Jesse Jackson pass for a vulture. A race-timid media have declared this big-butted bird a protected species, and it has gone to his head. He flaps around like the archangel Michael, but the Michael he most resembles is also the Jackson he most resembles. The one noteworthy difference between them is the glove.

As one of the least moral individuals in public life today, the Reverend Vulture is ironically one of the least vulnerable. He lives deep in a racial swamp of his own creation. When he's not defending convicted murderers, drug lords, street thugs, or third-world dictators, this vulture is managing a dozen different hustles and shake-downs to engorge himself, his family, and his friends. And by victimizing the very people he claims to be helping for nothing more than his own vainglory, this scavenger fuels the very racist myths that keep the swamp swampy and the black community indentured to the Democratic over-lords who would hate to see it drained.

Once upon a time, before he found a better racket, the Reverend Vulture ran Operation Breadbasket. Then he ran a couple of times for president. But now, as former D.C. mayor and convicted cokehead Marion Barry points out, "Jesse don't wanna run nothing but his mouth."

Well put, Mr. Mayor.

Scientists wanting to test which earthly phenomena

most closely approaches the speed of light can do no better than measure which reverend first reaches the scene of a racial flare-up, circling Al Sharkton or Jesse on vulture's wings.

Despite those wings, the Bush years have more or less grounded the Reverend Vulture. Without Bill Clinton and the Democrats occupying the White House, this vulture doesn't get to fly around Africa anymore and oversee such diplomatic triumphs as the one he and Wolf Boy engineered in Rwanda circa 1994. Nor does he get to pick the respective treasuries clean the way he did when he helped legitimize the strongman thugs in Liberia and Sierra Leone.

Nor can the Reverend help his buddies fly the coop as he did in the last few days of Clinton's term. If you recall, he secured pardons for one guy convicted of stealing five million dollars from the homeless, another convicted of sexually propositioning a thirteen-year-old, and worst of all, a guy guilty of serving several terms as a Democrat in congress.

Admittedly, Jackson and Bush got off on the wrong foot when he swooped down on Florida in 2000, surrounded himself with alleged Holocaust survivors from the local junior high, and claimed that Bush was trying to swipe the election. At that moment, few recognized the vulture's keen eye for things illegitimate, but by the time the inaugural rolled around, even the *New York Times* had to admit—after the *National Enquirer* forced them to—that the good Reverend had sired a little love buzzard. Make my year!

Who can forget those heady days during "the most ethical administration in American history," that eight-year-long summer of lust. And lusting is what Clinton and Jackson did, at least with their interns, if not their wives. Jackson's love mate was an employee who had written her PhD dissertation on Jackson. One can only imagine.

Apparently, Jackson chose to show her how Operation PUSH got its name, and the research quickly turned from sociology to biology. Jackson's generous ten thousand dollars a month research grant to the young scholar—not to mention the extra perks like $40,000 in moving expenses and the purchase of a $365,000 home—caught the attention of Jackson's employees, who blew the one thing not being blown: the whistle. Obviously, they didn't get quite as generous Kwanzaa bonuses that year.

Now this indiscretion would have politically clipped any other bird's wings, but with the *New York Times* writing articles like, "Moral Leaders Need Not Be Perfect," the Reverend Vulture was grounded for about a weekend. That's all it took for him to "revive" himself in the eyes of the media. Jim Bakker and Jimmy Swaggart may still be in semi-permanent timeout for their indiscretions, but not the Reverend Vulture. He had a corporate shakedown cruise to attend to—the "Wall Street

Project"—and neither an extortion rap nor a flock of love children were about to keep his sorry tailfeather out of lower Manhattan.

Tragedy struck lower Manhattan again on September 11, and once again, the Reverend Vulture swooped in to look for loose change. Within days, he reported that Afghanistan's Taliban leaders had requested his assistance to mediate this little dispute between their pathological country and the U.S. But when Mullah Omar's ambassador to Pakistan was asked about the request, he denied that the Taliban had initiated the contact. They likely feared that the Reverend was about to shake them down for the poppy concession. If he could squeeze the juice out of Chase Manhattan, they were already pulp in his hands.

"It is not important how the contact was made, but that the contact was made," said the rhetorically inventive Reverend Vulture of his would be Nobel Peace Prize gesture. Smooth move. It's clear that the Taliban's fear wasn't unfounded. Ever since his unsuccessful presidential bid in 1988, shakedowns have become the Reverend's specialty—corporations, countries, what's the diff? His "Wall Street Project" is known in the corporate community as the "Wall Street Heist."

A traditionalist, the Reverend Vulture brought his family members into the racket—excuse me—business. Faced with a choice between a national boycott and a franchise to half-brother Noah Robinson, Coca-Cola chose

"B," franchise. And days after Jesse picketed Anheuser-Busch in Chicago, his two sons were awarded the franchise there, one that nets this ravenous empire thirty to forty million dollars a year.

The Reverend never lets reality get in the way of a vigorous shakedown. In 2003, a Chicago nightclub—already under court order—burned down, killing twenty-one patrons. Within hours, Reverend "bloody shirt" Vulture and his legal accomplice, Johnny Cochrane, were threatening to sue the club owners on behalf of the families of the victims.

Oops. One problem. The Reverend apparently forgot just how extensive his fiefdom was. The owner's father turned out to be a cofounder of the Reverend's Operation PUSH, and the owner was a longtime Jackson family friend. The Reverend had even written to Chicago officials before the fire claiming that the club that burned down was "an example of the best that our business community has to offer." The *Old York Times* also found several ministers who had been instructed by Jackson to throw business to the illegally-operating club. In the end, what may have infuriated Jackson most was that his clan had not yet gone fully vertical and branched into mortuary services. Vultures don't like to leave any odds and ends lying loose.

The past year has kept the Reverend and the little buzzards buzzing. When he isn't wining and dining respected world leaders, like Kim Jong-Il of North Korea, Fidel Castro of Cuba, and Comrade Hugo Chavez of Venezuela, he has found the time to denounce the freedom movement in the Middle East. "Thomas Jefferson democracy has no export value on the international market," said the Reverend, and obviously not much in hometown Chicago either.

Closer to home, the Reverend Jackson swooped down on the dying Terri Schiavo when all that was left to salvage was a headline or two. And in the aftermath of Hurricane Katrina, this increasingly bottom-heavy vulture could be found flying around New Orleans, literally, looking for some Republican scab to pick.

Neither rain, sleet, or hurricane, will stop this scavenging, foul-weathered bird from following his predatory route. Because when this Reverend isn't praying (and it seems he seldom is), you can bet he's preying.

KiM JONG-iL

The Short-Necked Salamander is a stocky, pudgy lizard with sturdy limbs and a long, expansive, extremely dangerous tail. The body color of this sly creature is brown and irregularly marked with yellow to olive colored blotches. The only other salamanders with which it might be confused are the red Chinese variety and the Khmer Rouge (*rouge* being French for "red," which is the salamander's favorite color). There are thankfully few Short-Necked Salamanders left in the world today, for those that remain are a vicious, intemperate breed with a tendency to prey even on their own young and to threaten any species, large or small, that encroaches on their habitat. It might even drown a sibling or kill one of its own spawn if it feels threatened. But with an appetite for American blondes and Jack Daniel whiskey, while all of the other salamanders are forced to eat each other, the Short-Necked Salamander is one reptile that knows how to throw a party.

181

Kim Jong-Il is the political ayatollah of North Korea and, inexplicably, its current fashion statement (very odd considering this lizard looks like Rosie O'Donnell on a bad loofah day). This crafty creature assumed power after the death of his father, Kim Il-Sung, who took control of this deranged Stalinist country after we more or less kicked the Japanese out.

The North Koreans apparently worship the salamander like a demi-god, but it's not as if they have much choice. The one button on a Korean remote is on-off because this little reptile is the only show in town. Let's see: die horribly by torture or worship old Tiger Lily. I think I'll choose "B," says Jong Six Pack, at least until a better option comes along. It's fair to say most surviving North Koreans think Kim's a pretty special guy.

The multitasking Short-Necked Salamander is chairman of the National Defense Commission, supreme commander of the North Korean Army, general secretary of the Korean Worker's Party—which just happens to be the country's *only* political party—and head dog catcher, a coveted position comparable in power to America's secretary of agriculture. It's just that every trip of the animal control truck ends up at a Pyongyang restaurant. "Would you like some puppy-fried rice to go with your bowl of grass and tree bark?"

Needless to say, unlike in America, obesity is not a

real problem in North Korea. Not a problem at all, in fact. From the looks of things, the salamander is the only wide load in the whole country. He can't feed his nation of twenty-two million people because he himself has eaten everything that grows or moves or barks.

His father is as much to blame for the ongoing famine, having clear cut most of the country's trees to make room for rice paddies, endorsed by the party slogan, "Rice is Socialism." No one dared to remind him that the cool North Korean climate makes for poor rice cultivation and that cutting down all of the trees ensured that the rice paddies would be flooded over and made virtually useless. Maybe he wasn't such the "Great Leader" after all?

While his population starves, this lizard has assembled a large military, ostensibly to keep invading hordes from taking over the globe's most enduring example of a people's republic (and tellingly, it is just that, at least if we don't count Berkeley).

Some say that the Short-Necked Salamander's is the most obsolete large military force on the face of the planet, now that the Republican Guard is toast (literally), but word is that Kim believes there is a certain holistic virtue in hauling around his ICBMs in ox carts.

At one point, U.S. intelligence agencies believed the slick salamander had developed nuclear weapons, but the explosive test they were citing turned out to be a

German Shepherd he had left in the microwave too long.

It is unclear whether the salamander was formally educated in the Soviet Union, China, or North Korea, but judging by his spherical appearance, unusual in a reptile, it was probably at a university with a generous pizza bar. He is said to have majored in political economy, which would at least explain his government's current policy of putting politics before economy.

Kim Jong-Il has managed to make great progress during his tenure as the country's "Dear Leader." An avid environmentalist and backer of the Kyoto Treaty, he has done his best to end global warming by cutting traffic congestion to nil on the nation's streets and highways—you need cars and gas for that. Earth Day in North Korea is a year-long celebration. He has the whole country on a Slim Fast diet. He has banned casino gambling, lawn mowing, free speech, and underwear. And there's no MTV. A worker's paradise indeed!

As to unity on the Korean Peninsula, this lizard believes in the "Sunshine Policy" with the South. In particular, he agrees the North should someday unite with the South and, in the spirit of friendship, he has already thought of a catchy new name for the united peninsula: The People's Republic of North Korea. He has also generously offered to preside over this unified entity. In fact, he and the 1.1 million buck privates in a real "army of one" all but insist on it. This is one salamander who's not about to change his spots. No, sir.

The Short-Necked Salamander has kindly offered to share with the South his own helpful hints on sustaining what might best be called "political stability." Indeed, no other father-son dynasty, not even the Bushes, has ruled for fifty-eight uninterrupted years. And what with Uday and Qusay now distracted with their 144 collective virgins, that record isn't about to be threatened.

But Kim's climb to the top of the North Korean food chain required him to thin the family herd. First in line was his four-year-old brother, who "accidentally" drowned while playing with his older brother. Another victim of Kim's cull was his nephew, Lee Han-Young, who was assassinated in 1997 by a team of North Korean commandos in Seoul, even though he had undergone extensive plastic surgery to hide his identity. Lee's crime? He revealed that Kim had an illegitimate son in a book he authored after his defection.

But the father-son team of the "Great Leader" and the "Dear Leader" have thinned most other North Korean families by turning the state there into a lethal killing machine. One scientific study conducted in 1997 estimated that as many as 3.5 million people have been executed by the secret police, have been starved by socialist policies, have died in their gulags, or were killed in the Korean

War since the elder Kim assumed power in 1948. Apparently, the talk about reunification with the South is because the North is running out of people to kill.

Naturally, Kim Jong-Il has had rocky relations with the United States, with which, in fact, North Korea technically remains at war. He has insisted that his friends in the neighboring and peace loving People's Republic of China mediate any talks between the two governments— one, because the Chinese share his taste in cuisine, and two, because they aren't much more moral than he is.

As for the salamander's height, rumor has it that the five-foot-three-inch dictator often wears platform shoes, so as to appear taller and more intimidating to his counterparts. Shouldn't there be a height restriction to bearing nuclear arms? *You must be as tall as the clown's collar to ride the bumper cars and threaten world decimation.*

The Short-Necked Salamander has often been accused of being as much of a lady's man as his equally round and reptilian American kin, Newt Gingrich. They say that power is the greatest aphrodisiac—even the bespectacled, pear-shaped Henry Kissinger allegedly had a "stable"—which goes a long way in explaining Kim's appeal. Let's see: sixty seconds of tubby, fumbling sex play or death on the rack for my whole family. Hmmm, I think I'll choose "A."

And that's the real danger of this odd-looking lizard. Though just an insignificant little reptile in the animal kingdom at large, this salacious, salivating salamander rules his own tiny corner of the garden like he's king of the jungle, preening like a lion with his butch-cut mane, and prowling around the globe, ready to strike higher species with the same viciousness with which he rules his tiny reptilian world, just to prove his power—to become the Lizard King.

"John" Kerry
Flipper floppus

JoHN KeRRY

[Flipper floppus]

The Flipper family of Toothless Dolphins luxuriate in the protected coves of Cape Cod, Martha's Vineyard, and the South of France. This species has no established habitat or pattern of behavior but rather follows the prevailing current, usually in the shallowest water it can find. Thus, it has found the perfect home for itself in Wishy-Washington. When domesticated, the Toothless Dolphin is capable of performing amazing tricks, most notably the Double Flip Flop, which has both amazed and flabbergasted onlookers for years. Not particularly motivated to fend for itself, it has a talent for riding in the wake of creatures with deeper pockets, particularly females of the Flipper phylum. Scientists have recently discovered that the Toothless Dolphin is not as advanced in intelligence as the general populace once believed, ranking well below even below-average elephants, and less than the average donkey, hard as that is to believe.

189

Whether he's shilling for Al Jazeera ("young American soldiers" are "terrorizing kids and children") or pandering to MoveOn.orgasm (there's a "solid case" to impeach President Bush for "misleading" the nation about the Iraqi War), you can bet that when the political winds hit him in the tail, John "Flipper" Kerry, the Toothless Dolphin, will flip around like a weathervane and whistle *The Stars and Stripes Forever*.

Flipper has shown a remarkable, if unusual, skill in talking out of both sides of his mouth. He'll passionately argue one side of an issue before reading a poll, seeing a sign, or spotting a mackerel by moonlight and then passionately argue the other. Even his home state supporters in Massachusetts say they elect him for economic reasons: Where else can you get two positions for the price of one? Not even Eggo can match Flipper for waffles.

The man can't even make up his mind about going to work. He's spent less time on the Senate floor than Rush Limbaugh spent in college.

For all the talk of dolphin intelligence—*No one you see, is smarter than he*—Flipper is no credit to his species. It turns out that Flipper floundered at Yale, with a grade average rounding out to 76 percent, worse even than our unfairly maligned president.

So what qualifies this flip-flopping beast to swim to the head of his school? In a nutshell, he is the essence of what that school is all about. He is today's Democratic Party. *Generally*, he stands for everything; *specifically*, he stands for nothing. He's as solid as a meringue, as reliable as a Dan Rather newscast. It's best not to believe what he says because (a) he'll say the exact opposite tomorrow, or (b) it wasn't true in the first place.

Hey, give him a break, he's French—or at least he plays one on TV. In an odd linguistic twist, the French word for dolphin is *dauphin*, which also means "crown prince," a role that Flipper has assumed for himself since he was dorsal high to a whale.

You'll recall that in the 2004 presidential campaign, Flipper tried to portray himself as Joe Six Pack. Yea, if you mean a six pack of luxury homes with a collective price tag of more than thirty million dollars and another six pack of high end autos, including one of those environmentally friendly SUVs, and did we mention the luxury yacht? You've got one, Joe, right?

Don't think he didn't work hard for this. In the summer of 1962, while just an eighteen-year-old volunteering on Teddy K's first Senate run, he started practicing his upwardly mobile amatory skills on Jackie Kennedy's sister, Janet. In 1970, he married heiress Julia Thorne, split with her when she became clinically depressed, and after dating a few actresses, set his sights on bigger game, scoring ultimately with Teresa Heinz, the widow of Republican senator and gazillionaire, John Heinz.

Prophetically, Flipper met Teresa at an Earth Day. If you've seen his zombie bride, or merely heard her, you'd know he deserved every dime of his newfound fortune. How he must have wished that her words flowed no more quickly than her ketchup. That way, perhaps, they might have registered somewhere in passing.

If nothing else, however, Ms. Heinz taught the junior senator that—in a friendly media environment—there were 57 different varieties of answers to every question. In November 1988, for instance, at a businessmen's breakfast in Massachusetts, the aspiring comic said of the just elected president, "If Bush is shot, the Secret Service has orders to shoot Dan Quayle." In Massachusetts, however, embarrassing moments like this could be made to disappear quicker than you could say, "Mary Jo Kopechne."

Remember the controversy surrounding his medal-laden service in Vietnam? Flipper, seafaring as he naturally was, volunteered for the U.S. Navy. His reason, or so he said, "To whom much is given, much is required," a statement that endeared him to veterans everywhere, especially when he submitted a written request to be assigned to Vietnam. A safe, quick trip to Nam, he figured, meant a solid punch on his career ticket. There, according to some Swift Boat vets, he managed to turn an arm bruise and a self-inflicted piece of shrapnel in the tailfin to purple hearts, and his superiors dispatched him homeward before he got his uniform dirty.

Back home he learned that, in the blue states at least,

fighting wasn't the way to girls and glory; protesting was.
When this worm turned, so did Flipper. He told a Senate
committee that he knew soldiers who "personally raped,
cut off ears, cut off heads," of Vietnamese citizens and
rampaged across Vietnam "[razing] villages in fashion
reminiscent of Genghis Khan." Bad enough that he compared his fellow soldiers to Genghis Khan. What was really horrifying was that Flipper pronounced Genghis
"Zhengis" in a drawl so pseudo-aristocratic that it would
have appalled even his role model in the loving and leaving department, Claus Von Bulow.

The day after the hearing, Flipper threw his medals
over a fence at the Capitol in protest, except that they
weren't exactly his and they weren't exactly medals, and
who cares anyhow. "Did I tell you I fought in Vietnam?"

During the course of this protest season, he met that
treasonous tart, Jane Fonda, and marched with her arm-in-
fin. She had yet to make her millions in the exercise business, however, so Flipper chose not to marry her. Fellow radical Tom Hayden would soon claim sloppy seconds.

Turned on by the limelight, Flipper hoped to stay in
D.C. for the rest of his life. And since he had shot himself
in the butt and could say "Zhengis," tricks beyond the
reach of the average dolphin—*No one you see, is smarter
than he*—Flipper decided to start his career at the top.

Though not yet thirty, Flipper felt the world was just
about ready for Congressman Kerry. He just needed a seat

he could win so he started hunting for a "soft" district. Hiding behind the cloak of civic high-mindedness, his district shopping was so transparent that local pols dubbed it "Kerrymandering."

One local paper said that Kerry "has gone from the Third Congressional District to the Fifth, to the Seventh, to the Fourth, and now apparently back to the Fifth. One of the most irritating charges he has set himself up for regardless of where he eventually runs is political carpetbagging."

Happily for America, Flipper lost in 1972, but returned to Washington for good in 1985, this time as a senator. "I emphatically reject the politics of selfishness and the notion that women must be treated as second-class citizens." Whatever that meant, it got him elected. But remember this was Massachusetts. For the record, he didn't officially dump his first wife until after he had been elected, and at least he just dumped her figuratively.

Just a few months after arriving in D.C., Flipper and his fellow traveler, Tom Harkin, mamboed down to Nicaragua for a Sandinista suck-up. The newly-installed commies offered their new senator friends a deal. If the Sandies called a truce with the freedom-fighting Contras, would the senators try to kill all aid to the Contras? Said Flipper, "I am willing... to take the risk in the effort to put to test the good faith of the Sandinistas." The House killed the Contra aid, but on the very next day, Sandinista President Ortega flew to Moscow to accept a $200 million loan, turning Flipper's face as red as his politics. Now, the whole House flipped and voted a larger aid package to the Contras than previously offered.

Skilled international wheeler-dealer that he was, Flipper felt himself ready for the big time in 2004. In the run up to that election, he continued to exhibit a level of flexibility that, even at her most nimble, Barbarella couldn't top.

October 2002: Flipper votes *for* giving President Bush the authority to use his discretion in employing military force in Iraq. *Flip*.

September 2003: Flipper votes *against* an $87 million supplemental funding bill to support the war effort. *Flop*.

October 2003: Flipper tries to explain this flip-flop by saying "I actually voted for the $87 million before I voted against it." *Flip* again.

Trouble is, what Flipper is certain about he usually gets wrong. In his opposition to drilling in Alaska's ANWR, for instance, Dr. No said we'd only get "a few drops of oil" from the site. Hey Flip, try ten billion barrels—enough to power Massachusetts for a quarter century without going begging to Hugo Chavez.

And when the Toothless Dolphin's not blowing hot air out his spout, he's foolishly obstructing the political system, swimming in the way of presidential motions (such as Supreme Court nominations) that would otherwise cruise along smoothly. For instance, even after Democrats had conceded to confirming the qualified Samuel Alito,

Flipper flopped home from the Swiss Alps in a futile attempt to support a last-ditch filibuster. Kerry's international politicking was dubbed "Swiss Miss" by the Republicans. "This was the first time ever that a senator has called for a filibuster from the slopes of Davos, Switzerland," said White House spokesman Scott McClellan. "I think even for a senator, it takes some pretty serious yodeling to call for a filibuster from a five-star ski resort in the Swiss Alps."

Yet despite these fishy exploits, Flipper keeps getting reelected, thanks to the fact that in Massachusetts, he actually is the wiser and more honorable of the state's senators. This is the one state in America, after all, that chose George McGovern. Hugo Chavez could get elected there—and just might if he continues to buy votes.

The good news is that, in losing the 2004 election, Flipper may have tossed away his presidential future like one of those famed medals. Most people may not know this, but it's almost unheard of for a presidential loser to come back and win his party's nomination a second time (Nixon was the exception). And when they do, they often get beat again. Does anyone remember Adlai—*No one you see, is smarter than he*—Stevenson?

Perhaps we can all breathe a little easier that Flipper will be returning to the murky depths again, enjoying once more a life without porpoise.

LARRY KING

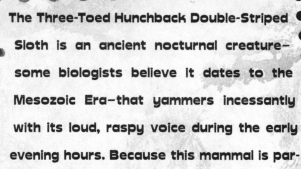

The Three-Toed Hunchback Double-Striped Sloth is an ancient nocturnal creature— some biologists believe it dates to the Mesozoic Era—that yammers incessantly with its loud, raspy voice during the early evening hours. Because this mammal is particularly unattractive and emits a sulphurous odor, as a result of its propensity for garlic ("the stinking rose"), the Hunchback Sloth spends much of its day scouring for willing females with which to propagate. Unusual among sloths, this one will "mate for life" innumerable times during its seemingly interminable lifespan. The Hunchback Sloth is known to get especially cozy with the Great White Brando, but is friendly with most Left Coast varieties of animals.

LARRY KING

Larry King's show reminds me of a trip to Graceland.
People from all walks of life—politicos, media stars, movie
stars, and murderers—make a pilgrimage to see the King,
even though he died almost thirty years ago. Oh, this sloth
may not quite be dead yet, but his career is—the FOX having surely killed it.

Yet it seems that everyone, at some time during the
respective downswing of his or her career (or after a stint in
"recovery"), goes on *Larry King Live*, an oxymoron if there
ever was one. The Hunchback Sloth may be many things,
but he's about as live as King Tut.

(Quick trivia question: Who was Larry King's first
guest? Answer: Moses—on the downswing of *his* career.)

Hunchback's show is a favorite stop for politicians and
celebrities alike because his questions are as unthreatening
as the three-toed sloth himself. Even his truly vile guests
like O.J. Simpson and Rosie O'Donnell—am I being unfair
to O.J.?—are thrown such softballs you'd think they were at
a Sunday picnic, not a "news show." One *New York Times*
columnist went so far as to call *Larry King Live* "the resort
area of American journalism, the media's Palm Springs,
where politicians and other figures of controversy or
celebrity can go to unwind, kick back, and reflect on what
a wacky and wonderful trip it has been."

Celebrities like the Hunchback Sloth, and the
Hunchback Sloth loves celebrities. In fact, this inglorious

King has kissed so many actors' rears and licked so many politicians' boots that he's lost all sense of taste. Hence such trenchant film reviews as: "Pure delight . . . I am in love with Herbie!"

Remarkably, this furry, slow-moving sloth can identify with any number of different species, including the most ferocious of the jungle. During the heady days of the scandal-plagued Clinton administration, the Hunchback Sloth could interview Bill and Hillary's friends and business partners with a straight face and a caring heart.

Larry King has shown time and time again that when it comes to his guests, he is less discriminating than even Art Bell. He welcomes nuts, cranks, and wackos with the same sincerity as presidents and prime ministers, regularly featuring interviews with psychics, paranormal "experts," UFO enthusiasts, and spiritualists. Among the regulars is John Edward, psychic and star of his own show on the Sci-Fi Channel, not to be confused with John Edwards, psycho and co-star of the short-running John-John show (also on the Sci-Fi Channel—as CBS was known during the campaign season). John Edward often talks to the dead while on Larry's show, but I guess that's being redundant. No one talks to John Edwards any more.

Perhaps the biggest crank to appear on King's show in recent years, though, was Walter Cronkite, or "The

Most Rusted Man in America." The "venerable" news anchor (who is, as a side note, one of the few newsmen older than King and about twenty years older than news itself) went on *Larry King Live* immediately before the 2004 presidential election and accused Karl Rove of setting up Osama bin Laden to make the videotape attacking President Bush released days before the election. Sure, Crankite, and Scooter Libby shot the video from the grassy knoll.

Larry also invited America's griever-in-chief, Cindy Sheehan, only to bump her right before the show for Michael Jackson. Wow, talk about insensitive. The protestor bumped for the molester. Did Michael Jackson ever lose a son? Heck, all he has lost is a nose, and he didn't lose that in Iraq.

It's generally all work and no play when the sloth's in the studio. Take for instance the recent interview he did with Nobel Biology Prize nominee Pamela Anderson, in which he asked thirteen separate questions about her breasts. You have to appreciate his journalistic thoroughness. Even though the questions may be soft, the Hunchback Sloth never is.

But when he's not in the studio, this surreal sloth can be found at his palatial estate relaxing with his wife of the moment, Shawn, playing with their two of his six children, or sitting at his desk writing alimony checks for his five ex-wives (six, if you count the one he married twice). Yes, the sloth is never slow when it comes to women and is a notorious serial monogamist, having been married seven times now. He says he loves marriage so much he keeps trying it over and over. He treats his wives like guests, bumping each wife if a better one appears.

One of this mammal's proudest moments came in 2005, when King received a "Father of the Year" award from the National Father's Day Council. Awarded, I suppose, for the way in which he spreads the love around. He has five children by four different women, one a "love child" by a women whom he never married, and a stepchild to boot. The Hunchback Sloth later commented that it wasn't often that he got to pal around with one of the other fatherhood nominees, Donald Trump.

Larry King and Donald Trump? Who did they give the "Mother of the Year" award to? Britney Spears?

Now having reached the twilight years of his career (and the ripe old age of 230), this TV legend can look back and think of the great moments of television history that he was a part of. Like when Marlon Brando leaned in and kissed the aging sloth on the mouth. Not so much as a sign of affection, I think, but in an attempt to eat him (the brisket was gone in the green room—Madeline Albright had just left).

Or those numerous times it's been reported that King (and here we get to the sloth's most disturbing habit) cut the cheese on the air. It's rumored that his audio technicians must keep King's microphone turned down, not to muffle the noxious fumes coming out of his mouth, but those emitted from his other end. The question is: Does he wear those suspenders to keep his pants from falling down or to keep them from blowing off?

And yet this valiant sloth soldiers on, his heart running on Energizers, his body stapled and stitched together and so full of hot air that it seeks spontaneous release, and he himself so deep in alimony payments that he could never even think of slowing to a slothfully respectful retirement.

No, the slow sloth must keep moving. And the snow job must go on.

Rush Limbaugh
Hushus bimbosis

RUSH LIMBAUGH

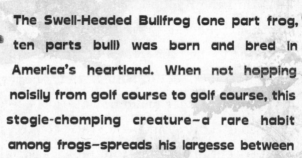

[*Hushus bimbosis*]

The Swell-Headed Bullfrog (one part frog, ten parts bull) was born and bred in America's heartland. When not hopping noisily from golf course to golf course, this stogie-chomping creature—a rare habit among frogs—spreads his largesse between two habitats, one in New York City and another in South Florida. Thought to be a frog of superior intelligence by frogs of inferior intelligence, this species transformed himself from a fat croaker in a little pond to a fat-headed croaker in a big one. In a strange freak of nature, the Swell-Headed Bullfrog feeds primarily on its own ego. Known to jump from mate to mate, an unusual trait among the subspecies conservatatus, this Bullfrog appears unable to keep the female of the species for any length of time. Happily, it has yet to reproduce, for it fears competition, even from tadpoles.

Rush Limbaugh (affectionately known to the Savage Nation as Hush Bimbo) is the rowdiest and was once the roundest critter in the GOP pet store. But while his belly shrank, his head continued to swell. Today, this frog and his copycats, Hannity and O'Reilly, are more loyal to the RNC than border collies.

Although he hates to admit it, Limbaugh owes his out-sized success to Bill Clinton. From Clinton's election in 1992 until the Republican Revolution in 1994, there was no other croaker in the red state pond nearly as loud or as irritating to the Democratic neighbors. For years, none of those neighbors could believe that one fat frog could do much more besides make noise—that is until 1994, when Rush chased fifty-four Democratic congressman and eight senators out of Washington, plus, as a real bonus, Mario Cuomo out of Albany. Rush seemed so loud only because he had a pitch perfect mastery of the croaks of his fellow frogs, many as irritated as he, but none quite so talented.

It has been an uneven hop since those halcyon days when the Swell-Headed Bullfrog first leapt out of his pond. Ever ambitious, he took a turn at TV but with his exaggerated, vaudeville-sized gestures, this modern-day Fatty Arbuckle quickly proved himself no Kermit. He had, as they say, a face made for radio. Even on the radio, the Bull Rush routine that was once fresh and entertaining had grown a tad stale and bland.

The old frog learned few new tricks. Now rich, he was no longer just another frog on the street, his ear attuned to the woes of his fellow toads, but a part of the Republican establishment. The bullfrog's most recent mishop came when his friends at the White House had him walk the lilypad on Harriet Miers's moronic nomination to the Supreme Court. While the Bushies were wringing their hands about Harriet's rapidly sinking ship, someone suggested that the bullfrog swim to her aid.

I can hear President Bush now: Quick, Dick, get on the red phone and call Limbaugh. Send out the EIB signal. This is a job for Fatman!

The Swell-Headed Bullfrog published an op-ed in the *Wall Street Journal* to no avail. Ten days later, Miers was back at her desk in the White House—thank God—and this frog's support was exposed as partisan bull. (Only Savage immediately saw Miers for the party apparatchik she was. I said on my radio show, "Why choose a nonentity when there are so many qualified entities!")

But Rush's true conservative credentials had been revoked long before that. Immediately following the weeklong love fest called the 2004 Republican National Convention, the bullfrog had to pipe up—again, in the pages of the *Wall Street Journal*—to tell Americans that yes, in fact, John McCain, Rudy Giuliani, and Arnold Schwarzenegger were really conservatives, even if from the tiny NARAL, gun-control, big-government wing of the party.

But it apparently didn't occur to Rush that when you have to defend the GOP's leftward shift, you have to redefine what it means to be right, and your fans know that's wrong. But today, alas, this bloated bullfrog seems more interested in dividends than principle.

Limbaugh has often been trumpeted as an amphibian of towering intellect, and that is true, at least in comparison to Hannity and O'Reilly. But that is a mighty small intellectual pond to be big frog in. OK, we know that Southeast Missouri State University is the Harvard of Southeast Missouri, but one floundering undergradute year there does not an Einstein make.

This bullfrog also champions family values. He just hasn't gotten around to practicing them. He's had more wives than original thoughts and no children, at least that anyone knows about—and we're sure the *Enquirer* is out looking.

In 1990, the still rotund Limbaugh pioneered computer dating—and probably photo shopping—as he met Marta Fitzgerald through Compuserve. He and the aerobics instructor exchanged bytes and soon enough rings, and Rush was now a three-time winner. Soon enough, he proved a three-time loser when he and Marta split. In 2004, Rush was reported to be dating and even engaged to CNN television personality Daryn Kagan (CNN + EIB = BIM-SPIN).

I don't know about you, but when I buy the pair a wedding gift (how about a matching pair of golf ball themed suspenders?) on go-around number four, I'm saving the receipt. They'll be separated, I suspect, before Larry King catches the bouquet.

Even more entertaining than the frog's mating habits is the ongoing story of his admitted drug abuse. Now, I'm not one to kick a frog when he's down, but Rush, for years, flatly condemned drug users. Once he got busted, though, he was croaking a different tune, and his defense of his behavior seemed to me at least indefensible. Surgery or not, having people purchase narcotics for you is illegal. And if this had been Sidney Blumenthal or James Carville, Rush would have had them boiled. Instead, he was getting boiled himself, and in his own hot water.

Rush puts the hypo into hypocrisy.

Of course, the chorus of hoots and catcalls from the Left were inevitable once Rush's misadventure had been revealed. But as with all things liberal, the lefties showed nothing but their own moral bankruptcy. They, after all, are the compassionate ones, the forgiving ones. Robert Downey Jr. has been busted more often for coke—far more often—than Rush has been married, and his Hollywood pals always have a part (and a party) for him when he "recovers." Hell, they should be sympathetic. Hollywood alone has put enough money into the coke trade to subvert several good size South American countries.

Having *Newsweek's* Jonathan Alter gloat about "bully conservatives" getting "a taste of their own bitter medicine" was also over the top. After all, how many of these mainstream media types have ever gotten stoned at their Grateful Dead and John Tesh concerts? If it had been Bill Clinton, they would all be editorializing about how everyone makes "special brownies."

And if Monica Lewinsky had kept meticulous records and blackmailed our former groper-in-chief for $120,000 only to later sell the story to the *National Enquirer*, just like Rush's maid did to him, these same liberals would have held press conferences on the South Lawn to demand prison time for her and a shutdown for the *Star*.

And when that fascist Florida prosecutor demanded Rush's medical records, there wasn't a peep of protest from the Air America crowd. There were no rallies in support of Rush at Berkeley or Bejing. Apparently, the Left is only concerned about patient privacy when it comes to Clinton appointees and their security clearances.

But maybe something good will come out of this debacle. Maybe the Swell-Headed Bullfrog will return to the swamp that spawned him and the principles that made him king of the pond. The world offers temptations, we know that, but the pond offers grace and peace. There, after a few humble years of low-cal, no-gloat humble pie, maybe his head will slim down to the size of his body.

Gwyneth Paltrow & Madonna
Skinun bonus & Strippus pretentius

MaDoNNa & GWYNeTH

[Strippus pretentius]
& [Skinun bonus]

The varying species of the Red Dodo, as exemplified by this young chick and old buzzard, are endangered in this part of the world and verging on extinction (or at least irrelevance). The Red Dodo's mating habits are indiscriminate and indecent, although the older of the species mates much more frequently and with much more exotic breeds. As the senior bird of this species ages, though, it tends to settle down, builds a nest and family, and will even take its younger counterpart under its wing, where it teaches its protégé how to desecrate its native habitat and defecate on sacred statues and memorials. The younger bird then nourishes itself on the elder's droppings. Both birds, however, adhere to the same migratory route, flying the American coop for grayer pastures, presumably because of England's reputation for great weather, terrific food, and world-class dentistry.

Let me start off by saying that these two birdbrains are not without talent. The problem is their talent is for saying the most absurd and embarrassing things, all the while deluding themselves that anyone above the age of twelve (or with a triple-digit IQ) even cares. Like most pseudo-celebrities that come of age politically in Left Coast green rooms, there isn't a college degree between them or even the wherewithal to get one.

If they were to combine all their post-high school credits into one resumé, they would be qualified for just three things: acting (as Paltrow has done credibly once or twice), singing (as Madonna has desperately tried to do several times), or saying, "America Sucks." Of course, their limitations have done little to stop their incessant chirping.

Here's a pearl from the Young Dodo, Gwyneth Paltrow, that Hollywood hypocrite whose "healthy" lifestyle keeps her looking like a *Survivor* survivor: "I worry about bringing up a child in America. At the moment there's a weird, over-patriotic atmosphere over there." Not in Santa Monica, honey, unless you count pledging allegiance to the Taliban. Yes, real patriotic spirit gets in the way of the requisite American self-loathing taught on the Left Coast.

And let's talk about that safe and secure environment in England. Since they banned handguns several years ago, violent crime has shot straight through the roof. Some areas of London now rival the bleakest neighborhoods of inner city America for deaths by firearms and well exceed American cities in assaults and street thefts.

But concerning herself with the real world would be too much for the reality-impaired Princess Paltrow. No, she has inherited her good looks from her actress mother, Blythe Danner, her connections from her director father, Bruce Paltrow, and her politics from Mao Tse-Tung as filtered through the cute guy at the Starbucks down the street. What, me worry? No, of course, not you. But let's face it, sweetie, without your parents' pull, you're a junior account executive at a Sherman Oaks ad agency, and your car dealer clients could care less about your limited worldview.

Instead of worrying about facts, this anorexic airhead has to use her few functioning brain cells to come up with a creative name for her daughter. Hmmm, let's see, how about "Apple." That's right, the Young Dodo and rocker husband Chris Martin dubbed their poor child Apple Martin, named, I hope not, after the fifth apple martini Gwyn was downing during her conception.

What's up with the way celebrities name their kids? Apple? Jett? Coco? Scout and Rumer? Phinnaeus and Hazel? They're children, you morons, not pets. Still, I'll bet my house against your lawnmower that young Apple is calling herself "Kathy" by second grade.

Oh, and for the record, guess where her child—whom she wouldn't want to raise in America—was born? In spite of living in England at the time, the Young Dodo returned to her "overly-patriotic" homeland to give birth. Why, you ask?

Enter the Material Girl.

When the Young Dodo's flighty exile mate, the Old Dodo Madonna (who has also flown the American coop for the rugged lifestyle of English manor house living), told her about the horrors of Britain's socialized hospitals, the Young Dodo decided to tuck tail to the U.S. to ensure a safe delivery. I guess the prospect of having to experience Britain's failed healthcare experiment outweighed the risk of having an American flag lapel pin stuck on her newborn's nappies.

Hollywood hypocrisy only goes so far, it seems. But that brings us to the Old Dodo herself.

If there's one person who's been able to overextend her fifteen minutes of fame, it's Madonna. While the bland, blonde Paltrow struggles to maintain one identifiable personality, the older of the species has lived through more incarnations than a suicidal Sikh. She has a knack for overhauling her persona at the drop of a conical brassiere and has somehow hoodwinked her fans into believing that she's gone from no-class American sexhibitionist to an upper-class English mother.

So why does this old bird keep doing new tricks?

Because, dodo that she is, Madonna is terrified of becoming extinct. She keeps evolving to keep from dying and has, therefore, fossilized before our very eyes.

And, unfortunately, her latest incarnation is the most grating: political and spiritual guru.

Really, what makes this geriatric stripper-cum-housewife think that anyone wants to listen to her scattered thoughts on Kabbalah—a mixture of Jewish mysticism and kooky New Age philosophy that has, supposedly, turned the Material Girl to Mystical Girl and Madonna to her newly appointed name of Esther?

Molesther is more like it.

She's also been known to use her multi-purposed mouth to offer political observations. In January 2004, the Old Dodo announced to anyone who would listen that America was a bigger threat to the world than Islamic terrorism. (Remember: "America Sucks.")

Imagine her dismay when, just a few months later, she was forced to cancel her tour to Israel because of civic unrest. It seems those pesky Palestinian freedom-fighters she loves to praise threatened to cut off the heads of her children. Yes, terrorism is far more inspiring when other people's children are getting their heads lopped off.

The Old Dodo then had to engage in the sport of choice among Left Coast politicos, hand-wringing. "Why do they hate me?" she cried.

Why do they hate you? Have you even listened to your

own God-forsaken music? Have you taken even a fleeting glance at your own depraved lifestyle? To their humble credit, these Islamo-fascists—and quite a few Americans, too—despise everything you represent. In many Muslim countries, women would be stoned—with real rocks—for the things (and people) you do before breakfast. Sean Penn. Warren Beatty. Prince. Dennis Rodman. Vanilla Ice. You've been intimate with more men than most proctologists, you've cavorted on stage like a stripper on crack, and yet you still have the audacity to ask why they hate you?

So both of these deluded ditzes, this bimbo-dodo-combo, continue to preside over their chicken coops and their hen-pecked husbands in the safety of Merry Old England. Except they found out last year that England is not as merry as it seems. After years of real hate speech, a few of the young and reckless took it out of the mosques and into the masses. And all of the ex-pat and Labor Party token Koranic verses did nothing to prevent the horrors of 7/7. Boy, I bet you dodos were glad you never had to take public transportation.

Yet the Young Dodo was even able to spin this display of cowardice into an opportunity to mock what she sees as silly American values. In the newspapers, she praised Brits because "there were no multiple memorials with people sobbing as they would have been in America." How dare she?! Didn't she feel the rage and grief that we all felt following the events of 9/11? Put little Apple on one of those buses, and see how stiff that upper lip stays.

This veteran of twenty-eight whole years of life experience is calling Americans overly emotional? Does she forget that the country she now calls home literally shut down for over a week of unbridled mourning when one of their powerless, pensioned princesses quit this earthly coil for Designer Shoe Warehouse Heaven?

Forgive my lack of irony, but this Young Dodo thinks anorexia is a fashion statement.

So, England, these two fowl-feathered freaks are your problem now. If you try to send them back, I'll return them and worse.

You think you got problems now. Wait until you get Miss Streisand.

Bill Maher

Loudmouthus Liberalitas

BiLL MaHeR

[*Loudmouthus liberalitas*]

The Southern California Screeching Weasel is a timid but noisy creature keen on annoying many of the other animals in the zoo. Although often posing as a predator, this weak, mostly herbivorous rodent has teeny teeth, no claws, shrunken reproductive organs, and wholly relies on the support of more productive animals for its meager existence. Its natural habitat is primarily the dark and smoky corners of little minds, but it has been known to venture into the light of respectable discourse until frightened back into its hole by bigger, more intelligent species. Its mating habits consist of noncommittal relationships with exhibitionist females. Because of its failure to either willfully or successfully reproduce, this pathetic little creature faces extinction.

The twisted reality of Bill Maher is seen in the basic premise of his two television shows, *Politically Incorrect* (cancelled in 2002) and *Real Time with Bill Maher* (currently on HBO), where he tries to marry the cynicism of pop culture to the real-life world of national politics. By randomly selecting four celebrities, pop icons, and actual political figures (the challenge is to tell them apart—here's a hint: the politicians are the less attractive of the dolts), the Screeching Weasel has created the perfect postmodern program where everyone's opinion counts, no matter how inane, bizarre, or flat-out crazy it might be.

Meet the Press meets the French Revolution.

But Maher's promise of equality is as empty as that of the French Revolution. His vision really isn't about allowing everyone to have his or her say. It's about fixing a fight where he can come in and cold cock unsuspecting victims. His handlers pick the predators and the prey in advance. The outcome of the show is about as spontaneous as that of *WWF Smackdown*. The regular losers being, of course, the poor saps who tune into his televised toxic waste.

Truthfully, the Screeching Weasel is the most annoying thing on television since static.

Thankfully, Maher was evicted from mainstream TV for his asinine "We've been the cowards" ramblings right after 9/11. In praising the bravery of the terrorists, that craven pack of murderers, the Screeching Weasel entered the self-hate sweepstakes before the contest got started, and corporate sponsors receded from the weasel's show faster than his rapidly disappearing hairline. Booted from ABC, he slinked away to the friendlier environs of cable TV, where the political talk-show circus had fewer rules and far fewer viewers.

Too easily impressed with his own forced cool, the weasel kicks around only the most kicked around of cows and flatters himself by calling them sacred. In a similar vein, he tried to elevate the tedious orthodoxy of his ABC show by calling it *Politically Incorrect*.

Of course, the Screeching Weasel didn't start off as the obnoxious, anti-religious televangelist that he is today. First he tried his hand at bad comedy, then moved into bad acting—has anyone seen *Pizza Man?*—before weaseling his way into even worse political commentary. Indeed, he makes Charles Grodin seem droll by comparison.

Maher claims to be a libertarian, which to him means a Bolshevik with a hookah. No lefty is left enough for this softheaded Soviet. According to Maher, the *New York Times* has no liberal bias. It speaks to middle America! Sure, if you draw America's western boundary at the Hudson River.

Yet despite pretending to be an independent, the Screeching Weasel regularly hosts Democratic Party fundraisers. He even got on his knees, along with guest and fellow traveler Michael Moore, to beg Ralph Nader to stay out of the 2004 presidential race lest he bleed off

Flipper Kerry's would-be progressive votes. What a sight. Most Americans pray to God. These two lefties hit their patellas to pray to a perennial loser who can't even drive a car and whose terrorist-coddling, closet Maoism couldn't get him elected mayor of Santa Monica. In the end, though, it didn't matter. Nader crawled back into his hole, Kerry crawled back to Massachusetts, and this weasel slithered on to his next gig.

Natural selection took its course.

As chairman of Politburo, L.A. Branch, Maher fashions himself as a modern-day Caesar, giving the thumbs up or down on his guests' political views. If you're a conservative Christian, according to the Screeching Weasel, you have a "neurological disorder" and believe in "fairy tales." The only true sins that are recognized in his world are patriotism and faith.

Of course, even about hypocrisy, he's hypocritical. A chronic quibbler about Second Amendment rights, the moment L.A. erupted in riots, Maher quit the quibbling pronto and got a gun. What's the matter, Weasel? Your lie-in-the-sky quasi-commie convictions not enough to keep you safe from the criminals your idiotic ideology spawns?

The most entertaining element of his show is the ongoing battle of wit with sharp-toothed conservative women. What protects Maher's ego is his failure to understand how painfully one-sided these battles are. Even former swimsuit model Kathy Ireland flustered the

Screeching Weasel by challenging his advocacy of abortion. Cut down by an aging supermodel! Hang it up, Bill.

The Screeching Weasel responds to his on-air emasculation by attacking conservative women who aren't there. Even though First Lady Laura Bush has never been on the show—and it's unlikely she ever will be—he felt free to compare her to Hitler's dog because she too loved her mate.

Screech also asked his guests to come up with a pet name for former First Lady Barbara Bush. America's oldest hippie, George Carlin, blurted out "The Silver Douche Bag" to laughing approval by Maher.

That's as funny as old cheese.

Will someone please tell me how Carlin keeps escaping from the rest home? And why do hosts like Maher keep booking this overmedicated old coot on their shows?

Maybe it's the best he can do.

This perennial bachelor hooks up with porn stars for girlfriends but refuses to settle down and rear the next generation of little weasels. Perhaps his aversion to reproduce is well and good given his understanding of children. "I have two dogs," Maher once boasted on the air. "If I had two retarded children, I'd be a hero. And yet the dogs, which are pretty much the same thing. What? They're sweet. They're loving. They're kind, but they don't mentally advance at all…Dogs are like retarded children."

Lacking children of their own, these weasels have to steal ours through the education and entertainment rackets. If they couldn't do that, they'd be trying to get the electoral franchise for Canine Americans. For these creatures, dogs are just like children, aren't they? "Why can't they vote?" they'll soon demand.

Whether it's Christians, first ladies, social conservatives, the mentally handicapped, or his scant audience, this balding weasel gets off by identifying the meekest and weakest of the herd and attacking, knowing full well he'd be devoured by any of the more aggressive species. (Savage has repeatedly rejected the producer's overtures to appear as a set-up for the weasel and his gang.)

Now I realize, as zookeeper, I can get hostile at times, but only because I deal with creepy predators like these all day. And because it's my job to protect tourists who just want to stroll through the political zoo without getting feces lobbed on their clothes.

So next time you see the Screeching Weasel targeting and striking some poor, hapless soul, let me know. I'll lock him into a cage that promises a more balanced contest. I'll pair him up with a female who could match him witticism for witticism, someone of equal intellectual heft.

Does anyone have Anna-Nicole Smith's phone number?

John McCain
Stockholmus blemishi

JoHN MCCaiN

[*Stockholmus blemishi*]

The Turncoat Mole is a crafty creature that is quick to switch pack allegiances without any observable reason to do so. It regularly eats from the lower ends of the food chain, but constantly harasses any other animal choosing to do so. In 2000, the Turncoat Mole was all but exterminated from the national scene when it tried to root itself into the hostile habitat of South Carolina. It retreated to Arizona and is now making gestures to go national once again. The Turncoat Mole sometimes hunts in tandem with the Senate snakes, with at least a few moles being eaten for dinner in exchange for looking bipartisan. Perhaps its chief natural weakness is that it is blind to how its burrowing undermines the principles of the party pack.

The Arizona desert is full of contradictions: beautiful, yet life-threateningly dangerous; at most times pleasant, and at other times, an inferno that rivals Hell. With that in mind, it's quite appropriate that Senator John McCain would represent the Grand Canyon State, because of the glaring contradictions that mark his personality and his political career. In fact, some now call him McKennedy, showing as he does the unlikely characteristics of someone who has an "R" next to his name, but who acts all too like a "D."

During the mole's Senate tenure, he has positioned himself on both ways of about every single policy issue. One day he is the king of special-interest conflict; the next, he's the outspoken supporter of campaign finance reform. At any given time, he can be a partisan Republican or a Jumpin' Jim Jeffords or a de facto Democrat. And when he swings over to the other side of the Senate aisle, he gives Republican cover to some of the most outrageous nonsense Democrats can concoct. Even the *New York Times* editorialized once that "bipartisan could mean 'supported by the Democrats and John McCain.'"

Despite this, the one question that haunts the Turncoat Mole's waking hours is: "Why don't Republicans love me?" Democrats love him; Independents love him; the mainstream media certainly love him. Why can't he get any love from the GOP faithless?

The first problem that the Turncoat Mole faces is that

he has become the dark diva on the right side of the aisle. Whenever he doesn't get his way, he storms to the nearest camera and breathes fire about how disgraceful his opponents are. Although his heroism was considerably more real than Kerry's, we are reminded that he was a POW in Vietnam so often that we all have exhausted our appreciation quotient.

Needless to say, the Turncoat Mole hasn't won many friends, particularly in the Bush administration. His attitude towards his colleagues and the members of his own party is what made the talk about a Bush/Mole ticket so ludicrous: Can you imagine him settling to be "vice" of anything? Hardly. The only way he would have agreed to be on the 2004 ticket is if Bush were on the bottom of it, or Kerry for that matter.

The hard feelings in the GOP towards McCain go back at least as far as the 2000 Republican primaries, when he got a chance to face the business end of attack ads. In typical turncoat fashion, this mole popped out of his hole and began pounding the base of his own party. After launching assaults on the perennial patsies Robertson and Falwell, calling them evil and then comparing them to notorious race baiters Al Sharpton and Louis Farrakhan, he was surprised that Christian voters turned out for Bush. How about that?

To correct that mistake, the Turncoat Mole seduced evangelical Gary Bauer into dropping out of the primaries and backing McCain's candidacy in return for paying off Bauer's campaign debts. All this accomplished was to assure that Christians thought as little of Mini-me (and he really is mini) as they did of Dr. Evil.

And then when the Turncoat Mole's primary campaign began to flag like Bob Dole without his prescription, he started hanging U-eys with the "Straight Talk Express." The Turncoat Mole would come out and say that he didn't think that *Roe v. Wade* should be overturned, and later in the day would say that he "misspoke" or was misquoted. And then while campaigning in the South, he did a full 360° turnaround by calling the Confederate battle flag "a symbol of racism and slavery" one day, a "symbol of heritage" the day after that, and, when the heat began to build, back to a symbol of racism on day three, completing the circle. But still he wails plaintively, "Why don't they love me?" Mole man, hate to break it to you, but they don't even like you.

One reason no one much cares for the Turncoat Mole is because when it comes to many of his public policy positions, he makes David Souter look like Ron Reagan. The campaign finance reform legislation he co-sponsored with Senate Democrat Russ Feingold set a land speed record in the unintended consequences category. Less than a month after the Mole/Feingold legislation went into effect, McCain had relegated it to the land of the living dead. If only it were merely dead and not stalking the land in spectral form!

And it's not like the Turncoat Mole was the poster boy for campaign finance purity either. Ever since he began his political career in the House of Representatives, he was beholden to some of the biggest influence peddlers in Washington.

Indeed, he launched his career of inspired bi-partisanship by emerging as the sole Republican member of the infamous "Keating Five"—a group of senators that tried to prevent an investigation into what became one of the silliest savings and loan bailouts in history. Keating had been a longtime political patron of the mole, helping to bankroll his first congressional campaign. If the Senate Democratic space head, excuse me, space hero, John Glenn hadn't been as deep in the scandal as the Turncoat Mole had been, he never would have been able to crawl out of his own burrow.

But even this brush with disaster didn't teach him much, as McCain became one of the most eager Senate recipients of campaign cash from some of America's most egregious companies: Global Crossing, WorldCom, Arthur Andersen, and Enron.

And since the passage of Mole/Feingold, he hasn't built a very good track record of following the very laws he authored. According to an investigative report by the

Orange County Register, in 2005 McCain cut an ad endorsing Marilyn Brewer in a California congressional special election. But the ad did not contain the disclosure at the end of the commercial stating the approval of the candidate—one of the chief features of the Mole/Feingold legislation. It was also revealed that one of the mole PACs was sharing phone numbers with the Reform Institute, a not-for-profit organization founded by the Turncoat Mole to raise awareness for campaign finance reform. Yet again, McCain has betrayed his own legislation that prohibits cooperation between PACs and tax-exempt nonprofits.

And the Turncoat Mole has lost the love of Republicans by playing Democrat on issues like gun control, tax cuts, Social Security privatization, and abolishing the Death Tax. During the campaign finance debate, Congressman Mike Pence went so far as to warn his Republican colleagues about mole legislation: "Any of you that are thinking of joining with John McCain on this issue should know that McCain is so deep in bed with the Democrats that his feet are coming out of the bottom of the sheets." And by "sheets," Pence was not referring to Senator Byrd.

The most recent betrayal is joining with Democrats as part of the "Gang of Fourteen" moderates in the Senate who want to control President Bush's judicial nominees. At one point, the Turncoat Mole threatened to block all of Bush's judicial nominees—including ones that

Democrats would allow a vote on—unless Bush appointed
one of his lackeys to the Federal Election Commission.

About the only thing the Turncoat Mole has not
betrayed, in fact, is his country, which is why he would
never make a very effective Democrat. But he's trying.
Like his attempt at the end of last year to undermine the
war on terror by attaching a rider to the Patriot Act reau-
thorization prohibiting the use of torture.

Admittedly, McCain knows a thing or two about torture. But one thing he ought to know is that it results in
the enemy giving you information, just like he gave it up in
Vietnam. Does he really expect us to believe that if a terrorist is captured and knows that his co-religionists of the
"Religion of Peace" are going to bomb the Biltmore Plaza
in Phoenix, that McCain wouldn't want all available tools
used to extract that information?

Suffering from the Stockholm Syndrome from his horrible years in captivity, enduring torture at the hands of
the Vietnamese sadists in the Hanoi Hilton, he now iden-
tifies with the enemy, eliminating our ability to squeeze
info out of enemy combatants. Joining the whinos on the
Left to ban "torture," the Turncoat Mole continued to give
up his already too liberal RINO non-identity. The
Turncoat Mole argued that our use of torture would legitimize the use of torture by our enemies. Yeah, like our enemies have ever had a problem torturing our captured

POWs. Isn't this just wishful thinking? Or is the mole just blind to his moral equivalency?

As hard as the Turncoat Mole has tried to burrow into the establishment, like working with Democrats to hold Bush's judicial nominees hostage or undermine the Patriot Act, the jackasses will never let him in. They don't trust war heroes who keep their medals. If ever this mole did get the Republican nomination, he needs to know in advance something about his "friends" in the media: They will be there, mallet in hand, ready to bop him in the head every time he tries to stick it out.

"I hate the gooks," McCain once said, "I will hate them as long as I live." They'll dredge that back up and more, Mr. Republican nominee. They'll make the Rocky Mountains rise from molehills like that one, and "rocky" won't even begin to do justice to the treatment you'll get.

BiLL O'ReiLLy

[*Lecherus leprechaunus*]

Top mammal in the Fox News pundit cage, the American Porcupine is a large terrestrial rodent well protected by its prickly exterior. When challenged, it erects its quills, swings its stout tail, and threatens to release the barbed tips into challengers' skin. Known for its grunting or groaning delivery, the porcupine is active mainly at night and is found occasionally on televisions in the sagebrush plains of the West. Also, according to legal filings that were "settled," the American Porcupine will occasionally try to find cable station staff willing to play games like "fetch the loofah" as part of its bizarre mating ritual.

Is Bill O'Reilly really an obnoxious, dictatorial jerk bent on hectoring and humiliating his guests to boost sagging ratings and his depleted self-esteem, or does he just play one on TV? Well, by all accounts, this American Porcupine is the real thing, a bona fide bonehead, crazy as a Fox News anchor, a real prick a thousand times over as only a porcupine can be.

Raising himself up from small media market news to become the guiding force behind tabloid journalism during his tenure at *Inside Edition*, there to be replaced by crack journalist Deborah Norville, this porcupine has become a trendsetter and an industry pioneer—at least in his own mind.

From his cage at *The No Spine Zone*, he lets loose like a porcupine on Percocet with his trademark smugness and patented sneer, regularly welcoming movers and shakers from the Beltway and beyond, threatening to boycott entire countries, barking nonsense about everything from the War in Iraq to the War on Christmas.

This newsy numbskull maintains that his dubious popularity is due to his (pardon while I clear my throat) "common sense" approach to politics and culture. No, Porky, I think people watch your show for the same reason they go to NASCAR races—to see the wrecks. In the world of serious political commentary, *The O'Reilly Factor* is no factor at all.

Here's an example of O'Reilly's "common sense" and

folksy wisdom: In the political blame game that followed Hurricane Katrina last summer, the leprechaun (or rather, *lepercon*) criticized Louisiana Governor Kathleen Blanco for not sending National Guard troops into New Orleans *before* the hurricane.

And just who was going to rescue the Guardsmen once the hurricane had come through? Shepherd Smith? You would think there would be at least a couple of renegade brain cells still fighting it out in that giant melon of his. Instead the porcupine's prickly noggin seems to be filled with nothing but platitudes and 1-900 numbers.

Yet the American Porcupine claims to be a registered independent, which is somehow supposed to suggest free-thinking on his part. I suspect, however, that his independent status derives from the fact that no one from left or right, the libertarians to the LaRouches, would claim him. This lepercon porcupine is so off-putting, he could turn a PETA-phile into a KFC franchisee. And yet, when-ever the American Porcupine needs some affirmation, he wanders back to the Republican pound, pays homage to his masters, and yelps for a treat.

If Hannity is the favorite son of the RNC, the one who makes mommy and daddy proud by dressing smartly and never saying a bad word about the family, O'Reilly is his cantankerous older brother. He may throw a barb or two about mom's meatloaf to prove his edgy independence, but he still lives in his parents' basement.

Few people at Fox wave the "fair and balanced" banner as mindlessly as O'Reilly himself, but as most people know, the American Porcupine confuses independence with incoherence. He refused, for instance, to invite author Ed Klein to discuss his biography of Hillary Clinton because Klein did not interview biographer *extraordinaire* Kitty Kelley for the book. He also bristled when Pat Robertson called for the assassination of Venezuelan Presidente Hugo Chavez, conveniently overlooking, of course, that he himself had called for the assassination of Syrian President Bashar al-Assad. Was he prickly because Robertson failed to footnote him? We're still waiting for the talking points memo to explain that one.

The American Porcupine even called your friendly zookeeper, Dr. Savage, a way-out "extremist" for demanding the bombing of Iran's ports. That is, until the lepercon himself called for the de facto nuking of San Francisco because of the insane antics of the city's Board of Stupidvisors.

He may seem like a poking, prodding would-be provocateur in the presence of politicos, but when in the company of ladies, O'Reilly morphs from porcupine to the big, bad wolf, huffing and puffing over the airwaves or telephone wires.

On his radio program, while discussing a lawsuit over New York City's policy of subway bag checks, the American Porcupine informed his co-host, Harvard Law-educated political commentator Lis Wiehl, that he was going to have to conduct a "full-body search" on her.

Careful, listeners, you're entering "The No Tact Zone."

And after a penetrating interview with mega-pornstar Jenna Jameson, this porcupine requested some video samples to do some further "in-depth" research on the issues that she had, ahem, raised.

And it was the occasion of his interview with Jameson's porn colleagues, Sunrise Adams and Savanna Samson, that got this porcupine the only attention he never wanted.

Apparently, with his quills at full alert after the interview, O'Reilly made an after-hours phone call to one of his female producers and described to her in graphic detail his vast collection of vibrators. Tapes of a subsequent phone call—in which the amorous porky expressed his enthusiasm for falafel and "loofah mitts"—made the Monica transcripts read like *Little Women*.

Here's what O'Reilly said concerning his fantasy of a Caribbean vacation: "Well, if I took you down there then I'd want to take a shower with you right away, that would be the first thing I'd do. . .Yeah, we'd check into the room, and we would order up some room service, and uh, and you'd definitely get two wines into you as quickly as I could get into you, I would get 'em into you. . . maybe intravenously, get those glasses of wine into you. . ."

What is it with guys named Bill? Between O'Reilly,

Maher, and Clinton, you have enough unfocussed libido to power (and populate) most Third-World countries.

And in the time that it takes to say "sexual harassment," both parties were in court, trading lawsuits instead of phone sex. Fortunately for the sake of Western Civilization, the pair settled out of court, and both are bound to a confidentiality agreement preventing any further discussion of the incidents. Even though they may never learn what a loofah mitt is, the world's billions breathed a sigh of relief. This was one sex story that even Fox News refused to hype. Good thing it didn't happen in Aruba.

Since settling the lawsuits, *The O'Reilly Factor* is more a No Skin Zone than a No Spin Zone. If nothing else, we can be sure that when his program contract expires in 2007, the American Porcupine won't be made head of HR.

But until then, a word of warning to all you ladies out there in the Savage Nation. If you phone O'Reilly's show during porcupine mating season, which lasts from about January to December, do your best to sound like Janet Reno, avoid the subjects of Greek food and cleansing devices, and, above all, steer clear of the porcupine's biggest turn-on, namely himself.

A porcupine in heat is a dangerous beast. If he loves you, you'll be able to count the ways. In fact, you'll be able to count 'em by the thousands while you pluck 'em the morning after.

NANCY PELOSI

[Leftus irrationalis]

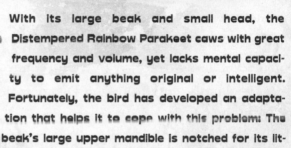

With its large beak and small head, the Distempered Rainbow Parakeet caws with great frequency and volume, yet lacks mental capacity to emit anything original or intelligent. Fortunately, the bird has developed an adaptation that helps it to cope with this problem: The beak's large upper mandible is notched for its little bird foot to fit in. Decked with bright blue plumage, the female of the species mates for life usually with strong and crafty males capable of building large nests and stashing a surplus of fruits and nuts therein. Not only does this preserve the pair from want, but also frees the female to spend nearly all of its waking hours bobbing through the jungle screeching at any animals not of its flock and pretending to care about those that have no nests and food at all. Although its original habitat was Maryland, the breed has since migrated to the San Francisco Bay area, where it aggressively climbed the political pecking order. Today it can be found both in California and Washington D.C., chirping away mindlessly in either environ. Curiously, aside from its lower-than-average intelligence, the parakeet suffers from one prominent congenital disability: It is only capable of flapping about in circles, primarily because it is born with only a left wing.

If by now you haven't realized that the chattering charlatan, Nancy Pelosi (or "Lugosi," to Republicans), is not the brightest bird in the rain forest, then you're dimmer than she is. Not that she's all feathers and no brains. In an impressive show of strategic intelligence, several decades ago the Rainbow Parakeet pecked out a wealthy and ambitious mate and hitched on to his green-hued tail-feathers in a flight from her native Baltimore to San Francisco. There, as the couple feathered their nest with a lucrative real estate business, she was able to pursue politics and develop a nicely feigned concern for the poor. The daughter of a Baltimore mayor, this parakeet set her sights on ruling the Democratic nest in a west coast habitat.

Amazingly, when she first ran for the House, she ran to the right of San Francisco Supervisor Harry Britt, but then again, as a gay activist and a member of the Democratic Socialist Organizing Committee, Britt didn't leave much room to the left. Over time, as her district grew gayer and grayer (thus, blonder), the adaptive congresswoman took on a rainbow hue.

Today as the House Minority Leader, Nancy Lugosi is the out-front representative for the Democrats in the House of Representatives. Politically, that's about as attractive as having Janet Reno represent Victoria's Secret, but who could disagree that this old bird has finally arrived?

As the chief parakeet on the perch, Nattering Nancy never lets an opportunity slide to squawk out a few passing shots at the political opposition. Tell her, for instance, that there's been an upturn in the economy and she'll chirp that it's at the expense of those who don't have jobs. An announcement of a new medical breakthrough will inspire her to cackle about its slowness in coming and the lack of universal health coverage.

For all her native color, she tends to think in black and white. When asked about a Democratic plan of action in 2005, she responded boldly, "Why should we put a plan out? Our plan is to stop him. He must be stopped." This discretion has nothing to do with valor because the "he" has nothing to do with Osama or al-Zarqawi. The "he" is her president—or at least our president. That "he" got 15 percent of the vote in her district. Even al-Zarqawi would have beat Bush in San Francisco. These wackos would go Sharia before they'd go Republican.

As the animal keepers here at the zoo have noted, unless the Rainbow Parakeet's beak is clamped, it's difficult to keep it from squawking. Not too long ago, this bird boldly proclaimed—apparently before checking with her staff, her congressional colleagues, or even the newspapers—that the war in Afghanistan was over. When she saw the jaws of the journalists in attendance hit the ground, she finally asked: "I assume the war in Afghanistan is over, or is the contention you have that it continues?"

The war in Afghanistan is over? I guess Pelosi "didn't put a plan out" on that one either. Wouldn't this world be a better place if our elected officials picked up a newspaper once in a while?

Also, last year when the U.S. Supreme Court ruled that state and local governments could use eminent domain to take nests of private citizens and turn them over to birds of a brighter feather, the Rainbow Real Estate Queen confused "could" with "had to." She apparently presumed that since it was the Court liberals who voted for this decision, they did so infallibly, as always. Not missing a beat, this parakeet loyally chirped that the Supreme Court decision was "almost as if God has spoken." For the Court's decision to be challenged, she insisted that a Constitutional Amendment was needed.

Imagine how the Rainbow Parakeet felt when she was reminded that hers is supposed to be the party of the little people and besides, the decision did not affect a state's ability to limit eminent domain. What's more, one particular state already had a law on the books to accomplish just that. What state was that, you ask? California. One of the few states that Pelosi had actually heard of and a portion of which she is alleged to represent.

And while Republicans sat in grateful, wide-eyed amazement at her appropriately parakeet-brained suggestions, even a Democratic staffer admitted to the Capitol

Hill press: "A generation of Schoolhouse Rock gets this and she doesn't?"

And if her current high perch is not enough to induce a national case of vertigo, imagine the state of affairs should her party retake Congress. The Rainbow Parakeet would most likely emerge as Speaker of the House, third in line for the most powerful position in the world's pecking order.

Whatever your misgivings about the people in power, I'd be down on my knees praying that Dickie's artificial heart keeps ticking. If this parakeet was ever allowed to turn the Oval Office into the Rainbow Room, you and I would be reminiscing about the good old days of the Clinton era.

Sean Penn

Peski apologista

SEaN PeNN

Native to the Left Coast, the Big-Beaked Toucan is a colorful, if perpetually ill-tempered, bird of paradise, born and bred in the protected environs of Hollywood. But unlike most toucans, this one is strangely compelled to migrate to war zones and disaster areas. While adverse to the glare of flashbulbs (hence the bird's notoriety for striking out at photographers), the Big-Beaked Toucan can deftly mimic the dove when in front of television news cameras. This particular breed of toucan gets its name from its decidedly large beak, perfect for tracking down bad scripts and sticking that giant proboscis where it doesn't belong.

Sean Penn, the toucan tough guy, has a long history of appearances in cinema. Unfortunately, like many of his Brat Packer cohorts, he is unable to distinguish real life from the fantasy of the characters he so gamely portrays in movies. Lately, he has tried to hoodwink the American public into believing that he is a bona fide reporter, an editorialist, and even a diplomat to Iraq and Iran! (Fortunately for the free world, it seems that so far he has limited his unwanted incursions only into countries that begin with the letter "I." Beware, Ireland and Iceland! This hawk-nosed dove may be flapping his way to a meaningless press conference in your country soon.)

Let's check the Big-Beaked Toucan's CV for any scintilla of qualifications that might lead him to believe he should be a spokesman for anything...except maybe misdemeanor domestic assault.

First, we discover that his first name is actually an anagram for "Stop! Enough Already, Nitwit!" Next, we find that after barely making it through high school in the mid-1970s, this odd bird enrolled in the Harvard of Santa Monica, Santa Monica City College, a two-year school where he studied auto mechanics. Apparently he was handier with a screwdriver of the Vodka variety than he was with a Phillips, though, because he failed to earn even an AA degree.

Also at this time, he dabbled in acting classes. Here's a bit of advice for you, Big Beak: If those acting classes weren't free, you should check the statute of limitations on refunds.

And there you have it: A failed mechanic who took some acting classes. So where does he get the chutzpah to think that he has anything moderately intelligent to add to any discussion of politics and public policy? As Truman Capote once said of Marlon Brando, "He's proof that you don't need brains to be a good actor." Big Beak is further proof, and he's not even that good.

Wait! Maybe the Big-Beaked Toucan owes his terrorism credentials to the fact that he studied history under the oppressive Mr. Hand in *Fast Times at Ridgemont High*. Or that he expanded his understanding of foreign intelligence by selling American secrets to the Soviet Union in *The Falcon and the Snowman*. And let's not forget how he honed his international diplomacy skills in *Shanghai Surprise*.

What, you didn't see that one? There's a shocker. I remember when that clunker came out. A guy called the theater box office, "What time is *Shanghai Surprise* showing?" Box office: "What time can you be here?"

This pompous poseur has had his hands in more bombs than an Al Qaeda operative. (Hey, maybe he is qualified to talk about terrorism after all.) I challenge anyone to sit through all of *U-Turn* without reaching for the remote . . . or the anthrax.

But still the Big-Beaked Toucan chirps on under the delusion that he actually has something important to say.

Actually, I'm glad the Left has chosen this birdbrain to carry its antiwar banner. He captures perfectly the great liberal mistake of confusing passion with intelligence— confusing *bad acting* with *good activism.*

This probably accounts for the $135,000 he paid the *New York Times* ("All The News That's Fit To Slant") and $56,000 to the *Washington Post* to run a poison Penn editorial stating his half-baked thoughts on the Iraq War. I don't know about you, but that seems like a lot of dough. He must still be getting alimony payments from Madonna.

Amazingly, the Big-Beaked Toucan doesn't always have to pay newspapers to print his flapdoodle. In some cases, they pay him for the privilege. The *San Francisco Follicle*, apparently unaware that journalism schools are graduating thousands of equally useful idiots per year, employed Penn to "report" from the Iranian elections. Shilling for the regime that wants to "erase Israel from the map" should, at least, net the toucan next year's Leni Riefenstahl award.

But at least the reporter-at-large-ego knew where he was reporting from. That's more than I can say for his fellow big-beaked cohort, Streisand the Barbarian. This high school-dropout-spokesperson-for-the-Left issued a statement that the dictator of Iran was none other than Saddam Hussein. Way to go, Professor. *People who need people* don't need people like you.

This is just more evidence of why I've placed so many

actors and celebrities in the Political Zoo. Like all thick-headed beasts, they all need attention. They need coddling. They need affection. But they also need handlers. And muzzles.

But it isn't just his movies and his political grand-standing that leave people cold. It's also his timing. Just days before 9/11, the Big-Beaked Toucan was flapping his wings overseas, applauding the violence and destruction committed by anti-capitalist rioters in Seattle and anti-American protestors in Italy. Then, from an ingrate who is protected by one of the finest police departments in the country while ensconced in his plush Marin County manor, this duplicitous lughead endorsed taking up "arms against the government."

Shortly thereafter, even when a group of sexually-repressed, American-hating Saudis with dirty nightshirts slammed fully loaded passenger planes into buildings full of American citizens, the Big-Beaked Toucan stayed his indecipherable course, refusing to condemn their actions. "I do not believe in a simplistic and inflammatory view of good and evil."

No, just a simplistic and inflammatory view of every-thing else.

You see, this bird doesn't prey, but espouses. He rejects violence and guns, yet when his car was stolen in Berkeley, he had to report that he left his handgun on the seat!

And unfortunately, it doesn't appear that the Big-

Beaked Toucan is in any danger of extinction. So I suspect that we will eventually become numb to his frequent squawkings and dismiss them as quickly we do those of his Queen Mother, Nancy Pelosi.

Still, he can be so entertaining. Nothing better exemplifies his out-of-control sense of self-importance than his post-Katrina excursion to New Orleans. This disoriented bird soared to New Orleans to save the huddled masses that he proclaimed had been abandoned by their duly elected leaders. Once in the Big Easy, he procured a dinghy—how appropriate—and set out to show America what one man can do. Well, actually two men. Even in the face of such destruction, Admiral Toucan had the presence of mind to bring along his personal photographer. ("Don't leave home without one.")

But he had no sooner launched the USS *Dunderhead* when it began to sink, and the intrepid Captain A-hole had to bail for his life with a plastic beer cup. It seems that our skipper was unaware that boats come with drain plugs, and it's best to check or replace them before shoving off on a three-hour tour.

As the Big-Beaked Toucan learned the hard way, when you are operating on a birdbrain, it's best to do so without cameras overhead.

Better still, his next announced movie bears the all too rich title, *In Search of Captain Zero*. And I didn't even have to make that one up.

Harry Reid
Mousi pugilisticus

HaRRY REID

[*Mousi pugilisticus*]

The Nevada Desert Kangaroo Rat earned its name from its repeated jumping from position to position and its rodent-like zeal for subversion and destruction. The Kangaroo Rat is one of the most lethal animals in the political zoo, not for anything it actually does, but for the progressive plague it spreads that is known to paralyze and destroy the body politic. Scientists haven't yet confirmed if the disease is caused by the special interest fleas carried by the rat, or if it's found in the odorous policy droppings that it leaves behind.

256

Harry Reid, the Senate minority leader, fights congressional corruption, battles special interests, and supports the war against America's enemies. Depending on what day it is. Or even the hour. For at other times, he promotes and conceals congressional corruption, rolls over in the face of liberal special interests, and supports the war against the nation's war to bring terrorists to justice. Thank heaven this tricky rat is only the *minority* leader.

For years, Reid was known as one of the "nice guys" of the Senate; and now that he has to try to play Mighty Mouse to the Republican majority, he does look a little uncomfortable trying to fill the void left by his predecessor, Tom "The Lobbyist" Daschle.

On a clear day, the Kangaroo Rat realizes why Daschle is now a member of the private sector: The good people of South Dakota finally realized that Daschle's body had been snatched by aliens from outer space only to be replaced by a liberal demagogue and obstructionist. The Kangaroo Rat's Democratic colleagues have a pod growing in his basement even now, just in case this bouncy rodent refuses to serve as the partisan liberal hack that Democrats need him to be.

The problem for the Kangaroo Rat is that the Democrats are not content to remain the minority party—hey, wouldn't you want a bigger cut of that lobbyist action?—and they won't give on their extremist policies and tactics. So they are asking Reid to do the impossible. Take for instance his attack on President Bush's justification for going to war in Iraq.

The fact that we're already several years into this war doesn't matter to Democrats who want to argue about the how and why it began. Also forgotten is that most Senate Democrats voted to authorize the war, including this fast-jumping rodent. Reid says now, "I based [my vote] on a number of things: yellowcake; aluminum tubes; secret meetings by Iraqi agents in Europe; training facilities in Iraq; training terrorists. All these things simply were not true." What the Kangaroo Rat doesn't say is that the information on which he had voted had been gathered under eight years of Bill Clinton and under two more years of the Clinton appointed CIA chief, George Tenet. And now he takes the word of those who told us that all of this is untrue from the same people who told us it was all true. Before jumping again, Kangaroo, wait until you actually know what you're talking about.

Plus, didn't the Senate leadership have exactly the same intelligence that the president had? That apparently isn't important. Neither is the fact that during the Iraq War authorization debate, the Kangaroo Rat gave an entirely different justification for his vote in favor of the war, saying that the Iraqis failed to comply with the cease-fire terms of the 1991 conflict: "It has refused to take those steps. That refusal constitutes a breach of the armistice which renders it void and justifies resumption of the armed conflict." That remains true, Roo. There are some things that even a Senate minority leader can't do, like wipe clean the congressional record.

Being conductor of the Senate Democrat "Bush lied, Qusay died" chorus isn't the only major position jump the Kangaroo Rat has had to make as leader. Last year, he likened Bush's proposal to allow younger workers to invest a small portion of their own Social Security contributions in the stock market to "gambling," a bit of unintended humor from a Nevada politician.

The Kangaroo Rat was hopping to another tune in 1999, when he said on *Fox News Sunday*, "Most of us have no problem with taking a small amount of the Social Security proceeds and putting them in the private sector." No concerns about gambling there, of course, because what he was talking about was allowing the *government* to invest Social Security money in the stock market. Of course, that's like having the state of Nevada place your bets at a Vegas roulette wheel. If we are too stupid to invest in the market, where most everyone wins over time, we are way too stupid to go to Vegas where most everyone loses.

And despite his attempt to squirm from the trap, the Kangaroo Rat is most assuredly captive to special interest groups, whom he cleverly calls "citizen's coalitions." During Supreme Court nominee John Robert's confirmation hearings, the Kangaroo Rat protested that he wouldn't listen to liberal interest groups, because they are "hard to satisfy." Of course they are. If they had their way, they would have put Hugo Chavez on the court. But that didn't stop the Kangraoo Rat from trying. He rolled over and played dead for those same interest groups—an impressive trick for any rodent—and opposed one of the most quali- fied jurists to be considered in the past century.

Reid was equally difficult during the recent Alito hearings, supporting a filibuster after having basically conceded to the inevitability of Alito's confirmation. The press secretary for the RNC put it best when she said, "Harry Reid's position on Judge Alito's confirmation has more holes than a slice of Swiss cheese"—something this rat knows only too well. "After stating an unwillingness to support a filibuster," she continued, "it looks as though the Davos Democrats were able to twist Reid's arm enough to switch him from 'Filibuster? Not me.' To 'Filibuster? Oui! Oui!'"

Nor is it just white male judicial nominees that he has trouble with. If you're a conservative black or Hispanic nominee, you should know that this rat is going to try to block you from even getting a vote. The Kangaroo Rat's most sophisticated tactic, learned from the master Democratic tacticians in the Senate, is name-calling, like when he described California Supreme Court Justice Janice Rodgers Brown, one of several black Bush nomi- nees he opposed, as "a woman who wants to take us back to the Civil War days." Right, Roo, that's because she secretly envies Aunt Jemima. "A problem" he said, is in the nominee's "confidential report from the FBI."

If you're lucky, you'll escape the treatment that judicial nominee Henry Saad received at the hands of the desert rat. During last year's debate over Saad's nomination to the U.S. Court of Appeals for the Sixth Circuit, the Kangaroo Rat violated a confidentiality agreement and discussed items from Saad's FBI background report in defense of filibustering the nominee. The trouble was that, according to Senate rules, only Senate Judicial Committee members and the nominee's home-state senators are allowed access to the file. The Kangaroo Rat, of course, was none of the above, but it's never easy to keep a determined rat away from the cheese. I guess there are some illegal leaks that Democrats don't have problems with.

"I think Harry Reid is lying. He's hiding behind something he knows he'll never be asked to show. Harry Reid is a coward." So said Saad friend, Michael Bouchard, sheriff of Oakland County. So what else is new? Bouchard, by the way, is "absolutely" certain that the FBI file doesn't contain anything damaging. But why let the facts stand in way of a successful smear?

And if you actually overcome all of the secret holds and other Senate rules trickery Democrats throw at you, rest assured that the Kangaroo Rat and his Democratic colleagues will vote against you, no matter how qualified you are, just like many did with Secretary of State

Condoleezza Rice and Attorney General Roberto Gonzalez. Aren't Democrats the affirmative action party?

The Kangaroo Rat has also taken a tough stand against Tom DeLay and his connections with lobbyist Jack Abramoff. Part of what troubles Harry about DeLay is that he kept some of his relatives on his campaign payroll. We don't want the appearance of corruption or nepotism in Congress, do we? But when reporters began digging through this rat's records, they found that two of his sons had received two million dollars for lobbying projects sponsored by the Nevada senator. In 2002, he introduced a measure to allow a private company to acquire 998 acres of prime Las Vegas real estate owned by the federal government without revealing that his son received $300,000 in consulting fees from the company to push the project through. He's the senator from Nevada for crying out loud.

And as for those ties to Jack Abramoff, the rat has some of his own. It seems that "Incorruptible" Harry received $66,000 in campaign contributions from Abramoff, his consulting firm, and his clients—money this rat refused to return, unlike his other Senate Democrat partners-in-crime. And while he denied any close ties to Abramoff, press reports indicated that the Kangaroo Rat's legislative counsel and assistant finance director for his campaign were hired by Abramoff, and those same staffers organized a fundraiser *in Jack Abramoff's Washington D.C. lobbying office* to raise campaign cash for their former employer. Well, we're all glad he doesn't have any close ties. More than a little hopping going on here, ay?

So while the Kangaroo Rat is busy jumping about, dodging questions about his family members who have stuck their snouts into the lobbyist trough, he has found the time to develop a strategy as the leader of his party in the Senate: more obstruction.

This is what got Tom Daschle evicted from the Senate, but the Democrats seem truly stuck on stupid. They've been kept in this zoo too long to even want to get out. They just want to eat the zookeeper. When asked by PBS news anchor Jim Lehrer if "success" for Reid meant "stopping the president from doing things rather than enacting things that you think should be enacted," Reid replied, "Of course, that's one of the things that I think is successful."

Hate to break it to you, Ratso, but Bush is the only one among you who doesn't need to run again. You, on the other hand, had better start now. For the voters are getting fed up with your double-dealing mousy ways, and should your constituents band together, as they should, they could become the pied piper of the populace and drive you and the rest of the rats out of Washington once and for all.

RoB ReiNeR

[Meatheadus nutcasus]

The Beverly Hills Meathead Bat sleeps upside down. As a result, over millions of years of evolution, the blood flow has resulted in a big, fat meaty head and the subsequent moniker, Meathead. Like many bats in its phylum, this one is a bloodthirsty creature that would suck the lifeblood right out of a taxpayer, draining him dry and leaving him for the recycling bin. This bald, rotund bat begins its lifecycle in the limelight of Hollywood but, as it ages, tends to migrate to the dark caves of politics, where it hangs with other predators, obliviously looking at the world upside down. The bat is blind to political realities but compensates by creating a fairy tale film world in which the bloodsuckers are always the heroes. This species feeds especially upon young families and children.

If you want to really see all the eccentricities of Left Coast liberalism in action, you only have to take a look at Rob Reiner. Just don't look too long. There's a reason why Hollywood executives are keeping this bald, ballooning bat *behind* the cameras these days.

Meathead worked his way up in Hollywood the old-fashioned way, by being the son of Carl Reiner, who actually had talent. Meathead's first major gig was not much of a stretch. He basically played himself as Archie Bunker's liberal, atheist son-in-law, Michael Stivic, a.k.a. Meathead, on the hit show *All in the Family*. The big and maybe only difference between Reiner's character and Reiner himself is that Stivic only appeared for thirty minutes each week and went away after nine seasons. We should have been so lucky with the Meathead Bat.

These days, the ungainly bat spends his time hanging behind the camera, where he has directed a number of films, some successful—*This Is Spinal Tap, The Princess Bride, When Harry Met Sally*—but lately, some decidedly not.

Said critic Roger Ebert of Meathead's 1994 classic, *North*, "I hated this movie. Hated hated hated hated hated this movie. Hated it. Hated every simpering stupid vacant audience-insulting moment of it." This was one of the kinder reviews, and one very good reason Meathead turned his humble talents to politics.

In that his father wasn't governor, Meathead has not been able to start at the top. As a heavy—in every sense— Democratic Party contributor during the Clinton years, he pretty much had to buy his way in. During the 2000 cycle, Meathead bellied up to Big Al Goreleone. By the time the presidential election came around, the two had not only become buddies, but Meathead had emerged astonishingly enough as a major policy advisor, more respected even than Ben Affleck or the Dixie Chicks.

Meathead traveled with Gore extensively, partly to warm up the crowds—he should have warmed up Al instead—and partly to make Gore seem slim by comparison.

Once Gore tanked, Meathead showed even more talent for picking losers when he helped bankroll Howling Howie Dean in the 2004 Democratic primaries. Since then, he has come home to the caverns of California politics. These are the nether reaches that he knows from boyhood and in which blindness is something of a virtue—or at least seems to be.

Gray Davis—the *North* of California politics—actually chose Meathead to lead a $700 million per year agency, the First 5 California Commission, a mammoth slush fund intended to provide care for children in the first five years of life. Meathead came by this post honestly, having been the primary financial and organizational backer behind the Proposition 10 initiative that created the agency in 1998.

In a gesture that would prove addictive, Meathead created a ballot initiative marketed by promising other people would have to pay for it. These were California's leper class, smokers, drawn disproportionately from the poor and powerless. They would pony up fifty cents more per pack to float millionaire Meathead's scheme.

Despite targeting only the lepers, the measure passed by less than half a percentage point. Under the Meathead administration, First 5 has spent only $1.3 billion of the $3.4 it has collected. But rest assured, $164 million has been spent on advertising. To keep this Hollywood bat's fellow predators busy, no doubt.

From his bureaucratic perch, Meathead has also decided to push through an initiative to fund statewide preschool for all four-year-olds, his worst idea since *Alex & Emma*, a movie that Roger Ebert kind of praised by saying, it "is not as bad as *The Story of Us*," yet another clunker from the mind of Meathead.

The most current Meathead initiative is drawing fire because it would put most private daycare centers out of business. Meathead wants to force any daycare that receives money to follow California's socialist union laws. But here's the beauty of it all. Guess who pays for advertising in support of the initiative? That's right, the First 5 California Commission, the very one Meathead chairs. This is what liberals think campaign finance reform should look like. Their causes get millions in taxpayer funding, which they control, and their opponents have to start from scratch. I don't see any conflict of interest in Meathead chairing the commission that pays for the ads promoting the private initiative he also chairs. Do you?

Archie Bunker might. I can hear him now, "Hey, Meathead, get your fat face out of my politics and your fat fingers out of my pockets. Make like Edith, you dummy, and stifle it!"

In an almost cinematic twist, this blood-engorged bat is now fighting California's hospitals. The hospitals want to increase the cigarette tax to $1.50 per pack to discourage smoking and to pay for emergency rooms across the state. Sound good? Not to Meathead. If people stop smoking, whose lifeblood will he suck? Who will pay for his commission? This bloodsucker finally found a tax he can't support and, in so doing, has driven a see-through stake right into the heart of compassionate liberalism.

Of course, all his political responsibilities have cut into Meathead's filmmaking time. So don't expect a *North II* or an *Alex and Emma: The Next Frontier*. As they say, there is a silver lining on every cloud. Still, California Democrats are trying to push him into running for governor in 2006 against Schwarzenegger. He has thus far declined after polls have showed the Terminator crushing his fat bat head in the general election.

When, one wonders, will Meathead and his bat pals ever see the light? The likely answer, alas, is never. Wrote Plato more than two millennia ago on the very subject of quitting the cave, "At first, when any of them is liberated and compelled suddenly to stand up and turn his neck round and walk and look towards the light, he will suffer sharp pains; the glare will distress him, and he will be unable to see the realities of which in his former state he had seen the shadows. . . . Will he not fancy that the shadows which he formerly saw are truer than the objects which are now shown to him?"

Watch out. Rumor has it that the Meathead Bat has already optioned *The Republic*.

Condi Rice
Stanfordus fiercum

CONDOLEEZZA RICE

[Stanfordus fiercum]

The Stanford Saber-Tooth Tigress is a fierce and calculating predator that stalks the Potomac swamps looking for senatorial prey, feeding almost exclusively on Left Coast Loons and the Marin County Dodos. There have been reported sightings of the Stanford Tigress all over the globe, and rumors that this friendly but ferocious feline has her cat eyes focused on becoming queen of the jungle. Do not let the cool demeanor of the Saber-Tooth Tigress fool you, though, for when you've got the power, and the ear of the pack leader, you don't have to growl.

272

Condoleezza Rice is one of the classiest acts inside the Beltway. Brilliant, personable, loyal, savvy, articulate, and inexhaustibly talented, she very well may be one of the most qualified individuals to ever serve as Secretary of State. She can even ice skate and play classical piano. Where did she learn all this stuff?

Kudos certainly go to her outstanding parents, both educators, for providing a stable and loving homelife and making sure that education was a top priority for young Condi. So serious were they about her education that her mother actually homeschooled (gasp!) her for a period to compensate for the horrible state of the Birmingham public schools (as if they've gotten any better years and billions of dollars later). It was this protective and deliberate nurturing in the den that allowed this tigress to sharpen her saber-teeth and grow to become one of the highest officials at one of the top universities in the world (Stanford) and one of the top political personas in America today.

Her academic credentials are as impressive as her many talents and her upbringing, and her presence as the chief defender of the president's foreign policy is formidable. You would never expect the Saber-Tooth Tigress to get cornered like Madeleine Albright did during her disastrous state visit to North Korea in 2000, when Half-Bright legitimized the sick Kim Jong-Il by being the guest of honor at a banquet where thirty thousand "volunteers" performed for her. Put Condi, George Bush, and Vladimir Putin in a room to discuss U.S.-Russian affairs, and you would find Vlad and W getting *her* coffee by session's end.

And yet, for all the grace and expertise she brings to her office, Rice has some very vocal detractors amongst the moonbat Left. Then again, you know the quality of the person by the enemies they make.

Take, for instance, the comments made by Banana Boat Harry Belafonte that likened Rice and Colin Powell to "house slaves." Right, like Belafonte's spent the last few years low riding with the Crips.

Within days, the Saber-Tooth Tigress was growling back, saying, "I don't need Harry Belafonte to tell me what it means to be black." No need to bite. I mean, all this tigress has to do is flash those intimidating teeth. When it comes to integrity, Condi wins hands down. While she publicly condemns the "outposts of tyranny," Banana Harry vacations there and pals around with the world's worst dictators. Maybe we need a Calypso revival to give this clown something to do.

Then there was the tigress's infamous showdown with Barbara Boxer during her 2005 confirmation hearings for secretary of state. Soon fur and feathers were flying, as the cunning Saber-Tooth Tigress proved herself to be the queen of the jungle, ripping apart the clueless Cackle Hen, making Boxer out to be the diminutive dilettante that she is—so much so that the day after Rice handed her brainless head to her, Boxer was whining, "She turned and attacked me!" That's what tigers do, chicken liver. It's in their nature.

Rice admits that she was driven from the Democratic Party into the ranks of the GOP by the incompetent foreign policy of Jimmy "I never expected the Soviets to invade Afghanistan" Carter. That notwithstanding, even Bill Clinton's top Russia advisor, Strobe Talbott, recommended that Clinton should appoint the prim but prowling tigress as the U.S. ambassador to Russia. He should have listened. She would later characterize Clinton's foreign policy with Russia as "happy talk." The ivy-covered halls of Stanford University weren't the only place where Clinton's foreign policy was considered a joke.

But the talk about Rice is no longer about mid-level White House NSC positions or diplomatic posts. She now runs the American foreign policy show, and as secretary of state, hopefully she will clean out the Augean stalls of Foggy Bottom—something her predecessor, Colin Powell, was unwilling to do. (Unfortunately, she recently attacked the Danish cartoonists for lampooning Mohammed. Not a good sign.)

Because of her visibility and her close relationship with President Bush, there's a lot of buzz about the fierce tigress appearing on the 2008 Republican ticket—

a prospect that puts Democrats in a panic. The reason most Democrats fear the Saber-Tooth Tigress is because they would have to find a new game to play other than "race card." She hasn't made her way in the world by racial quotas and affirmative action; she has achieved her success through hard work and self-determination— virtues she learned at home, not something she heard about at a college seminar.

Perhaps the biggest threat this tigress poses is that she has broken away from the slavish tyranny of Democratic plantation politics. No, Hillary, African Americans are working for you all. When you get 90 percent of their vote and have never given them anything more substantial than walking around money, that's a real political "plantation." Despite their party loyalty, they have not had a leadership position in the House or a place anywhere near a national ticket. If the Democrats lose that loyalty, the party is over. Literally. With those saber teeth, Condi could put a big bite in that vote, and that's got those jackasses staying up at night.

And remember, the Saber-Tooth Tigress doesn't come to the discussion of civil rights by way of a Banana Boat. When Belafonte was making his millions as a Calypso superstar (if such a thing is even possible), Rice was back in Birmingham. Two of the four children killed in the 1963 Birmingham Sixteenth Street Baptist Church bombing were childhood friends of hers.

In fact, recent polls for the 2008 presidential race show that she beats Hillary and John "Je me rends (I surrender)" Kerry in head-to-head match-ups, even though she has stated that she has no intention of running for president. Do you think that Hillary, Vietnam John, or Screamin' Dean want to make SAT scores a campaign issue against her?

The Democrats could put up any donkey they want in 2008, and the Saber-Tooth Tigress could have him or her (or Hillary) for breakfast. Although I initially thought she was over her head ("a little girl in Mommy's shoes"), I have to respect the energy and acumen she has brought to the Bush administration as NSC Advisor, and now as secretary of state. The brains and brawn that Condi brings to the foreign policy arena and to American politics are to be feared and respected. The growl of this tigress sends America's enemies running for diplomatic cover and the Democrats running for their political lives.

Bill Richardson
Speedae GonzaLez

BiLL RiCHaRDSON

[Speedae gonzalez]

The New Mexico Roadrunner is the kind of bird that would rather run than fly, although, as shall be seen, it can adapt when it needs to. The Roadrunner is one of the fastest creatures in the Southwestern desert and can easily outrun a human, which it often has to do. Fueled by the natural gas created by its ample diet of small snakes, lizards, mice, scorpions, and insects—although "diet" in this particular case is a bit misleading—the Roadrunner can reach amazing speeds, which allows it to dodge and flee hazards, as celebrated in the Warner Brother cartoons. It has become a cause of national concern due to its passage through and into the Los Alamos Nuclear Laboratory, which creates unseen openings for the dreaded Chinese dragonfly to infest the facility. The Roadrunner is also occasionally a food source for the "coyotes" who bring illegal immigrants into the United States.

As one of the serious contenders for a spot on the 2008 Democratic presidential ticket, Bill Richardson, the current governor of New Mexico, keeps track of the political winds better than a New Orleans weathercaster. Defender of the Clinton administration flame, globetrotter and grandstander extraordinaire, and all-around Democratic blowhard, the Roadrunner was on Al Gore and John Kerry's short list for VP nominees in 2000 and 2004. But the list is never quite short enough to accommodate Richardson's spotted resume. The candidates just need to have someone who looks vaguely like a minority to pacify their indentured minority supporters.

Besides, don't think for a minute that the Roadrunner would ever be content to playing Shallow Al Gore in someone else's administration. He would more likely play Roadrunner to the president's Wile E. Coyote. This guy is starved like a North Korean peasant, but (as is obvious in his case) only for media attention.

Not all of Richardson's press has been pleasant. The Roadrunner was Clinton's U.N. ambassador. Ron Brown had turned it down because he thought it a "minority" job, except he used a little rougher word than "minority." The speedy Roadrunner mostly just dodged bullets while the co-presidency of groper-in-chief Bill Clinton and commander-and-thief Hillary Clinton, craving the attention and recognition of foreign diplomats, surrendered America's foreign and domestic policy agendas to the socialist straw men of

Old Europe. The Roadrunner is also the one that praised Saddam Hussein's "compassion" in his own book.

The Roadrunner's best foreign policy performance as U.N. ambassador was his negotiations with Fidel Castro to open the country up to American trade at the instigation of the Cubans, who asked repeatedly to meet with Richardson. After granting concessions in return for the release of some Cuban political prisoners, Comrade Fidel tested the bounds of his newfound friendship by shooting down two Brothers to the Rescue planes. These planes were piloted by four Americans, who were killed in the shoot down. To placate the Cuban dictator after his murderous outburst, Clinton's chief U.N. diplomat offered to put an end to the Brothers flights, which had saved countless numbers of Cuban refugees trying to escape the brutal Castro regime. As Elian would later prove, for the Democrats, Cuban Americans don't count as "minorities."

In light of that record, it is somewhat ironic to note that the Roadrunner is also the Democratic Party front man on immigration. You can tell it's him by his quick movements and sudden reversals on the issue. In 2003, he welcomed a busload of illegal immigrants on their way to protest U.S. immigration policies in Washington by saying, "Thank you for coming to Sante Fe. Know that New Mexico is your home." Imagine that, the Roadrunner playing kissy face with the Coyotes.

But last summer, as the private initiative of the

Minutemen put a stranglehold on immigrants crossing the border from Mexico, and the PR worsened for illegals, the Roadrunner and fellow Democrat, Arizona Governor Janet Napolitano, declared a state of emergency regarding the border situation. The Roadrunner then lambasted the Bush administration for not demonstrating "the commitment or the leadership to deal with border issues." Bush could start by throwing Richardson in jail.

What kind of leadership has Speedy Bill shown in trying to stop the flow of illegal immigrants? None whatsoever. In his 2004 Spanish-language Democratic Response to the State of the Union address, the Roadrunner complained that Bush's immigration policy "does not help immigrant workers to obtain the golden dream: legalization and residency without impunity." He went so far as to call a Bush proposal to build a barrier fence along the U.S.-Mexican border "anti-immigrant." Isn't that the point of a fence, to keep illegal immigrants out? Nothing can apparently escape the gravitational pull of the Roadrunner's black hole mind.

So what is Richardson's solution to the illegal immigration problem? The same failed Democratic policy that has been tried repeatedly and been found wanting: amnesty. Rather than addressing the illegal part of the equation, he would just declare everyone legal. What genius! What a way to discourage future illegals.

Even less impressive on the Roadrunner's resumé was his role as Clinton's secretary for the Department of

Energy. In this capacity, he oversaw one of the most massive security breaches in American history when China stole hordes of U.S. nuclear secrets from the Los Alamos DOE lab—in his home state of New Mexico, no less. As the awful truth of how much classified material was leaving the lab became public, the Roadrunner tried to get in front of the issue by firing back at accused traitor Wen Ho Lee's charge of racism. Lee "unfairly tried to use the race card," said the Roadrunner more than a wee bit disingenuously.

The Roadrunner had done exactly the same earlier in the scandal. He tried to block the release of the congressional Cox Report that detailed how far the spying had compromised U.S. nuclear security by saying that "those who have questioned the patriotism of Asian Pacific Americans are also sowing the seeds of a darker xenophobia."

Yes, for the Roadrunner it's all about the race, and Richardson plays the race card like an ace up his sleeve. Truth be told, he's built his entire career on this shifty tactic. If his mother had been Croatian rather than Mexican, he'd be running for the Albuquerque school board, not the presidency. His "minority" status is his only discernible political asset. Credentials like an affluent Anglo Citibank father and attendance at all the best East Coast schools and colleges—at least the best that he could get into (Go Jumbos!)—do not play quite as well in the barrio.

In good Clintonian fashion, the Roadrunner's tenure as New Mexico governor has gone from scandal to scandal. He sexually harassed his female lieutenant governor to the point that she admittedly refused to sit or stand near the Roadrunner during public events to avoid his groping. (Now that's what Clinton would call a "hands-on" administrator.)

The Roadrunner soundly beat his Republican challenger in the 2002 gubernatorial election by promising to cut personal income taxes to "promote growth and investment." But just like any liberal tax cut scheme, the devil was in the details. An analysis of his tax cuts, most notably the elimination of the tax on food, showed that all of his tax cuts were offset by tax increases in other taxes and fees. In reality, his tax cut was really a $178 million tax hike—a tax cut any MoveOn.org supporter could love.

And the Roadrunner comes by his nickname honestly. On several occasions during his first term, the Roadrunner's life in the fast lane has been exposed as his gas-guzzling SUV has been caught burning up the New Mexico asphalt. In 2003, a *Washington Post* reporter was with him when the Roadrunner told his driver to go faster, even though they were traveling in excess of 100 mph. And just last year, the Roadrunner's detail refused to pull over for a state trooper that had clocked them doing 110 mph on a side road as Speedy Bill was tending to a state emergency—trying to get to a dinner hosted by Sen. Joe Lieberman.

The Roadrunner, to his credit, has responded to the public criticism by telling his driver to slow down, and also by authorizing the purchase of a $5.45 million Cessna Citation

Bravo jet and commandeering a $3.8 million state police search-and-rescue helicopter to cut down on his drive time. In fact, the helicopter is now used as much to ferry the Roadrunner's entourage, including his taxpayer-funded etiquette consultant, to public events as it is to track and capture felons—one of its primary tasks before the Roadrunner's land speed record attempts.

The Roadrunner has already made his intent known to run for president in 2008. His campaign will surely center on his extensive, if dubious, resume as congressman, diplomat, cabinet secretary, and governor. But missing this time will be his ancient claim to have been drafted into baseball's major leagues, after the *Albuquerque Journal* found that Speedy Bill had never been drafted by the Kansas City Athletics. He has made this claim for decades, likely thinking that no one would challenge a draft by a team as lame as the Athletics.

Even his response was pure Clintonian: "After being notified of the situation and after researching the matter . . . I came to the conclusion that I was not drafted by the A's." The Roadrunner travels so fast it appears he's left even his memories in the dust.

In fact, about the only thing this Roadrunner remembers is where the cameras are located. As nimble as he is, and as evasive as he has been, the one thing the Roadrunner will never dodge is the limelight.

Pat Robertson
Propheticus evangelicus

PAT ROBERTSON

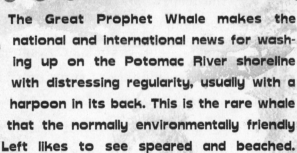

[*Propheticus evangelicus*]

The Great Prophet Whale makes the national and international news for washing up on the Potomac River shoreline with distressing regularity, usually with a harpoon in its back. This is the rare whale that the normally environmentally friendly Left likes to see speared and beached. Every bellow or random spout attracts a veritable navy of media Ahabs all obsessed with jabbing this great white God-fearing mass of blubber. Despite the best attempts of the Prophet Whale's friends to push the animal back into the sea and into obscurity, the media dependably gather for each re-beaching, and this attention seems to attract the Prophet Whale to still another disastrous contact with the banks of the Potomac. Although media in America may prize this leviathan for its entertainment value, certain less civilized nations (such as Venezuela) have no restrictions on its hunting, arguing that it does so merely as an act of self-protection.

The son of a Democratic senator from Virginia, Pat
Robertson, the Prophet Whale, made a wrong turn as far as
the media were concerned, when he changed in that D for
an R. From that moment on, he was fair game.

Knowing his vulnerability, the Prophet Whale's allies
have tried to keep him out of the political circus, it not
being a suitable place for a whale in any case, and he
knowing fewer tricks than even the average whale. No,
they would rather steer this sometimes disoriented beast
back into the deep, where no one notices or cares what or
how often he spouts.

But this persistent whale keeps washing ashore, be it
running for president or running from criticism.
Whatever current the whale follows, however obscure it
may be, the media monitor its every shift in direction as
though the current or the whale really mattered. They
record every bellow, hoping they can edit it into something awkward or even damning. And sometimes they succeed. Never, though, has a single animal with so little real
power been so closely watched.

When the Prophet Whale made a quixotic run for president in 1988, the media vetted his war record as though
he already had his finger on the red button. In fact,
Robertson served in Korea during the Korean War as a
U.S. Marine, an appropriate branch of the service for a
seagoing mammal. The media, however, invested more
reportorial zeal on his war record in this oddball candida-

cy than they would on John Kerry's, who actually ran as a war hero in his serious run for the presidency. The question was whether the Prophet Whale actually saw combat, with more reporters pillaging his files than voters punching Robertson's ticket.

The fact that Robertson had a whale of a career as a preacher, a broadcaster, educator, and an entrepreneur, let alone as a U.S. Marine, mattered not at all. That he got his law degree at Yale, the same university that hatched Bill and Hill, earned him no credit either.

How could it? Isn't he the same whale that spouted off about feminism, allegedly calling it a "socialist, anti-family political movement that encourages women to leave their husbands, kill their children, practice witchcraft, destroy capitalism and become lesbians." In truth, he said that this was what "the feminist agenda" was "about." And if he meant by killing children, killing their unborn children, I am not sure I know why we're supposed to be embarrassed by this. After all, it seems his prophetic vision is realized more and more each day.

Nor does it matter that the Prophet Whale is an outspoken friend of Israel. In 2002, the Zionist Organization of America gave him its *State of Israel Friendship Award* for his unwavering support of Israel. That same year, the Coalition for Jewish Concerns publicly thanked Robertson for "unwavering support for Israel" and "standing up to evil."

The media work to keep this info under wraps, and there is a specific reason why. For years, the Democratic National Committee has frightened scores of thousands of little old Jewish ladies out of their retirement money with the threat of a neo-Nazi rightwing Christian theocracy led by the likes of this amiable spouter. If you just read their junk mail—which is everything the DNC sends—you'd think that the only thing that keeps this whale from splashing right up onto Miami Beach and eating every Mah Jongg player in sight is the DNC and its wholly owned subsidiaries like the Southern Poverty Law Center (SPLC) and the Anti-Defamation League.

The real tragedy of this strategy, beyond creating an unnecessary rift between Christians and Jews, is that while our liberal vigilantes remained in a state of high dudgeon about a nonexistent threat, Islamofascists were meeting openly and plotting to kill Jews and other Americans, which they surely succeeded in doing on September 11. On that same fateful day, among the scores of "hate groups" listed on the SPLC watch list, not a single one was Islamic. These old folks' money would have been much better invested on bingo cards or new Mah Jongg tiles.

OK, I'll be the first to admit that our whale does occasionally put his flipper in his mouth and maybe even more than occasionally. But unlike our friends on the Left, the Prophet Whale has never rejected his own country, never attacked another race, and never sucked up to Hugo Chavez. In fact, he has done quite the contrary. In late 2005, in a provocative bellow even for him, the Prophet Whale said, "I don't know about this doctrine of assassination, but if he thinks we're trying to assassinate him, I think that we really ought to go ahead and do it. It's a whole lot cheaper than starting a war, and I don't think any oil shipments will stop." Many of us agreed with him.

They don't call this prophet a killer whale for nothing.

ChuckSchumer
Gotham pushus

CHUCK SCHUMER

[*Gotham pushus*]

The Brooklyn Jackass is an obstinate and excessively loud beast of burden that was removed from the petting zoo by veterinarians for turning overly red when petted. One should approach this braying creature cautiously. If it is near a camera, be particularly careful: Never place yourself between the ass and the lens. A particularly volatile animal, the Brooklyn Jackass has to shift its position when exposed to light or heat. It is closely related to the dumbass and often carries out the simplest tasks ass backwards. (Not related, as some think, to Ruth Gator Ginsburg.)

Though stubborn as the name of his breed implies, Chuck Schumer has made himself a powerful player in the Democratic barnyard, serving as one of its chief Senate spokespeople, donor pocket-pickers, and party-line enforcers. With both him and Hillary Clinton in New York, some have suggested license plates read "The Vampire State."

Schumer's love/hate relationship with his own Senate Democrat colleagues is an indicator of how frequently his ego gets in the way of his politics. The typically sedate Bob Dole once famously quipped, "The most dangerous place in Washington is between Charles Schumer and a television camera." Even former Senate Democrat and now New Jersey Governor John Corzine was forced to admit: "Frankly, sharing a media market with Chuck Schumer is like sharing a banana with a monkey. Take a little bite of it, and he will throw his own feces at you."

It's true. It doesn't take a crowded media market to get the Brooklyn Jackass to start flinging the feces—a difficult feat for a hoofed beast in any case—as any Bush administration judicial nominee could tell you. Even though the Brooklyn Jackass has never worked a day in his life as a practicing attorney—in fact, he may be the only person in Congress to have never held a real job of any kind—he wields his seat on the Senate Judiciary Committee the way Lester Maddox wielded his ax handles—keeping "those people" out ("those people" being anyone who believes in the Constitution).

And how the times have changed. When Republicans were opposing Bill Clinton's judicial nominees, Schumer complained that all nominees should get an up or down vote, but now he's almost singularly responsible for trying to use the judicial filibuster against Bush judicial appointees. Indeed, Beltway denizens have taken to calling this obstructionist practice "Schumerize."

You can't say that he lets his principles, such as they are, get in the way of his constituency either. In the weeks after 9/11, the Brooklyn Jackass brayed in the pages of the *Washington Post* that the terrorist attacks inaugurated a new big government era, a "new, New Deal." And he delivered a deal for New York. He and Hillary pushed through a $21.4 billion bailout for New York City and have since asked for another $20 billion, even though investigations by the press have found that very little of the original money has actually gone for 9/11-related expenses.

The Brooklyn Jackass has also delivered for Senate Democrats as the head of the Domesticated Animal Senatorial Campaign Committee (DSCC), which regularly raises more money than its Republican Senate counterpart. But even though this ass might be on the Judiciary Committee, don't talk to him about the law when he's trying to get more Democrats elected. In one of last year's unsung scandals—in Washington, "unsung" equals Democratic—two of Schumer's DSCC research opposition staffers illegally obtained the credit report for Maryland Lt. Governor Michael Steele, an African American who is presently the leading Republican contender for the Senate seat being opened up by retiring Democrat Paul Sarbanes.

Now mind you, these staffers were just doing their job, trying to keep Steele out of the "plantation." But as with all political crimes, the only real transgression is getting caught. In fact, the pair were caught posing as Michael Steele, which was the only way they could obtain the report. It just so happens that their "research" was a federal crime, and the FBI is still investigating the matter. But don't worry; Uncle Chuck was there to protect them, no *Time* covers, no CNN, no confessions on Oprah even. The pair was placed on paid leave while an internal "investigation" was conducted (like anyone there believed they hadn't done it), and when they were forced to resign, the DSCC still hired and continues to pay for their lawyer. It was all in good fun for a good cause.

That being said, the Brooklyn Jackass remains one of the most vigilant senators on the issue of identity theft, even serving as chief sponsor of the Schumer-Nelson ID Theft Prevention Bill. Hypocrisy, thy name is Schumer! Just as it was with Bill Clinton lying about sex to a grand jury, digging up dirt illegally on your political opponents was really just a case of boys being boys. As in Pinocchio, though, the penalty for such boys, over time, is to turn into donkeys and get shipped off to Bad Boys Island. In a pinch, Riker's will do.

If you think this was the end to the jackass's mischief, you obviously don't read the news much (and who can blame you?). While the Brooklyn Jackass was one of the most eager proponents of campaign finance reform, in 2003 he was slapped with one of the Federal Election Commission's most massive fines ever for his 1998 campaign. In addition to paying a $130,000 penalty, he had to return another $120,000 that he had obtained illegally. It might be hard to believe, but even in Washington, $250,000 is still a lot of money.

Still, the Brooklyn Jackass takes his role as the head of the DSCC seriously. He even exploited the tragedy of Hurricane Katrina to raise money for Senate Democrat campaigns. Just days after the hurricane struck, in the spirit of bipartisan cooperation, the DSCC posted an online petition asking people to call for FEMA Director Michael Brown's resignation. But in order to sign the petition, the DSCC website immediately directed you to a page asking for a donation.

And just who was pushing his Democratic colleagues out of the way to get to the microphones to denounce the leak that Bush-critic Joe Wilson's CIA desk jockey wife was behind his scavenger hunt to Niger? The same jackass who had voted in 1982 as a congressman *against* the Intelligence Identities Protection Act he now was claiming as sacrosanct. And why did he oppose it back then? So government whistleblowers, just as in the Plame case, wouldn't have to fear about spilling secrets to reporters.

Being one of the Second Amendment's worst enemies doesn't stop this ass from traveling with armed bodyguards around Washington and New York, two cities whose strict gun laws would seem to make armed guards unnecessary. Besides, when was the last assassination attempt on a senator? The average NYC cabbie runs a far greater risk, and he doesn't get to travel with a posse like the good senator.

Happily for him, the Brooklyn Jackass has the mainstream media to cover his tracks on his "do-as-I-say, not-as-I-do" position on guns. For instance, CBS News ran a story in 2001 about a lawsuit against a gun manufacturer. This manufacturer made weapons that would be banned under any gun law that Schumer has proposed. CBS showed a picture of the weapon being used at a range, but it conveniently cropped out the picture of the shooter—the Brooklyn Jackass himself.

And yet, the senator has surprised this zookeeper by being more vigilant on national security than the president! He led the charge to block the sale of six U.S. shipping ports to a company controlled by the U.A.E. While Bush and company defended this transfer of control, including port security to an Arab company, Senator Schumer had the foresight to block the sale! Politics *does* "make strange bedfellows," indeed!

"Arnold Schwarzenegger
Terminatus strudelhead

ARNoLD SCHWaRZ eNeGGeR

[*Terminatus strudelhead*]

The Terminator Rhino, or RINO (Republican in Name Only), is a large, primitive-looking mammal that uses its protruding anterior horn for horning in on any number of things for which it is neither equipped nor qualified. The indigenous habitat of this thick-necked animal has been severely threatened, but successful RINO reintroduction programs have been established in political reserves in California, New York, Maine, and even Rhode Island in order to replenish the American herd. This particular RINO Rhino has been the subject of many films and documentaries, in which the awkward beast utters unintelligible catchphrases before sending its enemies to quick and gruesome deaths (while disappointed audiences beg for the same sweet release). The RINO Rhino is almost always in heat (and on occasion in *Red Heat*).

With his tough protective hide, Arnold "The Terminator RINO Rhino" Schwarzenegger looks very much like the Republican elephant. But don't be fooled. This fierce-looking, muscle-bound beast turns into a ninety-pound weakling when it comes to defending conservative principles. On screen, it's all *Terminator*. Off screen, it's more of the same *True Lies*.

Though native to Austria, this lumbering beast has shown remarkable adaptability in the land of opportunity, making at least three major career changes in his fifty-eight years. He moved from big-time bodybuilder to big box office film star before finally transitioning into big mistake politics (the one place where his dreadful acting abilities and cornball slogans could actually gain him accolades). With only a slightly better grasp on the English language than George Soros, the RINO Rhino has become governor of the most populous state in the U.S. He follows in both the prestigious tradition of actor-governor Ronald Reagan and the preposterous tradition of muscle-head-governor Jesse "the Body" Ventura.

Which leads us all to ask: How in the heck did this happen? Back in the mid-eighties, while watching Schwarzenegger in *Commando*, garbling one of his lame tough guy lines (like "I eat green berets for breakfast, and right now I'm very hungry") can you imagine thinking, "One day, that man will be governor of California"? It could only happen in California where art rarely imitates life, but where life never ceases to imitate bad movies. I only wish I could walk out of California (when I didn't like the show), complain to the manager, and get my money back.

So how did the Terminator Rhino horn his way in to the political zoo? Well, one of this creature's shrewdest maneuvers was mating with a female of the purest liberal pedigree, Maria Shriver, NBC news reporter and queen ascendant of the Kennedy kingdom. By becoming an in-law in America's most flawed political dynasty, the RINO Rhino maxed his political visibility and viability. And as an outspoken Republican, he seemed downright sane in comparison to Hollywood's often comic insanity. This also furthered the RINO's image as a one horned maverick.

President G.W. Bush launched Schwarzenegger's political career by naming him to the President's Council on Physical Fitness and Sports. Although not much of a stretch, the appointment gave him the chance to expound his political philosophy in prestigious political journals like *Muscle & Fitness* and *Flex* ("The only thing you have to fear is flab itself!").

But his real opportunity at political glory came in 2003 when a recall movement threatened to unseat the sitting (or more accurately, squatting) California Governor Gray Davis. Myth has it that rhinoceroses can stamp out fires, and this RINO believed it. When he saw the raging fire of economic chaos consuming California, he moved to terminate it.

In so doing, this odd toed beast led the charge for Gray Liberation. He laid out an agenda for California that promised to reverse many of Davis's destructive policies and to roll back taxes to their pre-Gray levels. Gray, having played the state's energy market like a Keno Wheel, had proven to be the Golden State's biggest flop since *Gigli*.

Still, despite his enormous popularity, the RINO proved to be a strange candidate. In trying to communicate his vision for Kal-ee-forn-i-a through his thick Austrian accent, he sounded like a cross between Heinrich Himmler and the Tasmanian Devil, mangling his words as if they were renegade androids. Joining his crusade to the capitol was a rogue's gallery of the weird and the useless: Arianna Huffington, former baseball commissioner Peter Ueberroth, *Hustler* magnate Larry Flynt, surly Lilliputian Gary Coleman, watermelon-smashing has-been Gallagher, and even porn star Mary Carey. To the rest of America, the recall was a novel distraction. To California, it was business as usual, including a storied Hollywood ending in which the action star cleans out Dodge. But his victory was, as it turned out, not exactly a triumph for Republicanism.

It seems the steroids-in-a-drum that the Terminator had been spreading on his Wheaties for the last four decades came with the usual side effects: dwindling brain cells and weakened vision. His ties remained red, but his heart was turning blue.

The Terminator Rhino expressed his support for gun control (except, of course, when needed to blow away cyborgs or aliens—and only those of the outer space variety). He has also voiced support for abortion and medical marijuana. Hey, when you lie down with yellow dogs like the Kennedys, you wake up with flea-bitten ideas.

In 2004, the conflicts between the Republican governor and the Democratically-controlled California State Legislature finally came to a head. To break governmental gridlock, the RINO Rhino backed four ballot initiatives to restructure state government and effectively put an end to the Democratic stranglehold. But as he learned, it is easier to dispatch a cyborg than to defeat an energized union, and all four measures lost. Why? Because the core conservative base abandoned *him*, not the ballot measures. Their absence was a protest against *his* absence from core conservative principles.

Isn't it great to have such a tough guy in charge? Alas, the RINO Rhino has played at governor with little more finesse or conviction than he played at Conan the Barbarian. He even lured Gray Davis's former chief of staff—a lesbian who "married" her lady friend in happy Honolulu—to appease the abortion-sodomy lobby. Now, the distortionists in the media are claiming this rhino's ratings have improved, because he "moved to the center." As usual, they just made this up.

They say that the RINO is an endangered species. They say that its habitat is shrinking and its numbers are dwindling. Let's hope they are right. Because too many of these lumbering creatures have stumbled to the left. And the peculiarly lopsided Schwarzenegger variety, with his muscle-bound biceps but flabby spine, is no exception.

Al Sharpton
Pompadouro buffoonum

AL SHaRP TON

[*Pompadouro buffoonum*]

The Megamouth Shark, also known as the Sharkton, is one of the most feared creatures of the east coast, though relatively harmless to humans (despite the media's excessive, sensationalized coverage of "Sharkton Attacks!"). Although the Megamouth Shark spends most of its time roaming through its natural habitat—the polluted bays of New York City—its species will migrate to anywhere there are rough waters and vulnerable swimmers. Fortunately, it is easily spotted by its dorsal fin that looks very much like slicked-back hair. The Sharkton can smell the odor of cultural tension or race being baited from miles away, but though it often threatens to attack other species, it usually preys on its own kind. Natural enemy is the Great White Anything.

Maybe it's just me, but whenever I see Al "the Shark" Sharpton appear on the scene of some political event or racially-charged situation, I swear I can hear the *Jaws* theme playing in the background. Protest march in Bensonhurst. Demonstration against NYC cops. A run-of-the-mill race-baiting Democratic primary or presidential campaign. Wherever there's even the faintest scent of controversy, the low brass rumblings of John Williams' eerie score kick in, and the Sharkton is sniffing blood and ready to strike.

Where do you even start with this rank fish? I guess at the beginning . . . with the "reverend" part. Just for the sake of comparison, let's see how the Sharkton stacks up with some other prominent men of the cloth:

Rev. Martin Luther King Jr.: B.A. from Morehouse College; three years of theological study at Crozer Theological Seminary. Earned a fellowship to Boston University, where he was awarded his Doctorate in Divinity at age twenty-six.

The Right Reverend Bishop Desmond Tutu: Graduate, University of South Africa. Ordained Episcopalian priest in 1960 at age of twenty-nine. Studied theology in England, which led to his Master of Theology degree.

Reverend Sharkton: Preached his first sermon at the age of four. Fully ordained minister in the Pentecostal

Church at age nine. Ten years later, he took general classes at Brooklyn College, but left after two years to join the James Brown College of Musical Knowledge as Tour Director and pompadour-double.

A minister at the age of nine? Who ordained him, Ned the Wino?

If the Sharkton is a man of the cloth, then it must be polyester. Even the vilest of accusations, virtually all of them true to the letter, don't stick. Just look at this guy's track record.

His first foray into the political arena was in high school. He protested against the cafeteria food. What, wouldn't they serve thirds? Then, at the ripe old age of fifteen, he was appointed—by Jesse Jackson, no less—as youth director of Operation Breadbasket, a provocative lure and dangerous posting for a man of his appetites.

The ir-reverend went national in 1987 when he took up the soon-to-be lost cause of Tawana Brawley. This fifteen-year-old claimed that six unidentified white men—some of them police officers—raped and assaulted her and then covered her with feces and scrawled racial slurs across her body. From the media's perspective and the Sharkton's, this was just typical white guy behavior in New York State in the late 1980s. Once the Megamouth Shark bit into this case, it was pure feeding frenzy.

Of course, none of it was true. But the truth has

never stopped the Sharkton and his roaming pack of predators. They kept moving. They even accused a New York prosecutor of being one of the six and left his bloodied reputation behind in their wake. Brawley later admitted making up the story, but the Sharkton never apologized. He kept roaming the rough waters, looking for his next prey.

He found it in a relatively trivial rent protest against Freddy's Fashion Mart in Harlem, which led to an appalling mass slaughter when the Sharkton and his National Action Network called down an anti-Semitic tirade against the proprietor. This inspired one of his deranged henchmen to burn the store down, murder seven people, and shoot several more. When taken to task for his role in this felony, mildly at that, the Sharkton denied even being there. That was, until a videotape proved otherwise. Caught red-finned, all Al could say was, "What's wrong with denouncing white interlopers?"

What is astonishing is that none of this has dimmed the career prospects of this slippery predator. Hillary still takes his calls. When he mans the dais with his fellow Dems in a presidential debate, no one has heard or seen any more than the witnesses at a Little Italy rub out.

It is the Rev's latest endeavor, however, that brands this slickster trickster as an exploiter extraordinaire, and the most ruthless shark in the sea. The Sharkton recently cut a series of commercials for LoanMax, a Georgia-based pay-day lender that targets poor, and primarily black, borrowers for high-interest loans secured by the borrower's car! The interest rates—or "vig" as Tony Soprano might say—are so high they're actually banned in New York and dozens of other states. Many carry effective interest rates of 30 percent per month. To carry a $400 loan for a year would end up costing a whopping $1440!

"When I'm out fighting for the little guy," declares Sharkton in the ad, "and I need quick cash, I find comfort in knowing that LoanMax is here for me."

It's a good thing this pompadoured buffoon is there to protect his black brothers from whitey. But who'll protect them from the Sharkton himself? A hundred percent interest rate? This shyster must think it's Jimmy Carter time all over again.

Now, of course, if this were Chase or CitiBank charging these kinds of interest rates to poor people, Reverend Al and his pal Jesse Jackson would be screaming from their pulpits that this was still another Jewish conspiracy to keep a brother down. In fact, Reverend Al attacked these kinds of unfair lending practices before a Federal Reserve board meeting in 1999, where he argued for "loans that are not at rates that are unbearable and not set up with clauses that are unachievable." One member of the Congressional Black Caucus, Rep. Stephanie

Tubbs-Jones, went so far as to say that "predatory lending is the civil rights issue for this century."

But I guess such predatory actions are OK as long as you're the predator. Sharpton's been a political shark, a race shark, and now a loan shark. So what's next for this enterprising "interloper"?

I've got an idea. How about the reverend becoming a pool shark?

Sure, he could insinuate himself into the pool halls of the inner city, take the name of "Ministerial Fats," and hustle poor little kids out of their food stamps.

Now, if he could only be sure that his friendly dorsal would still be a welcome sight in the Hamptons.

Cindy Sheehan
Bearus twistus

CiNDY SHeeHaN
"SHaMe-HaM"

The Thin-Coated Dancing Bear is native to California, where she once roamed peacefully with her family without attracting any notice. But while mourning the loss of one of her brave cubs (the noble U.S. Army Spc. Casey Sheehan by name), the Thin-Coated Bear was seduced by an unscrupulous crew of dancing masters who taught her how to tango to their tune. Though never learning to dance with much skill or dexterity, rapt audiences have flocked to see this sideshow routine, amazed that such a bear could dance at all. The dance that this bear has performed might best be called the Hate America/Bush Bash. Millions of left-leading dancers perform the Bush Bash throughout the world, most of them much more skillfully, but since few others had lost a cub in "Bush's war," this Mother Bear has become a special if suspect attraction.

I approach all bears cautiously, especially one who has
been so wounded. Some critics might hate me for taking
on this particular breed. But my critics already hate me,
so here goes.

Let me start by saying that the one great tragedy in
this world is when a parent has to bury his or her child.
And contrary to rumor, Cindy raised this cub with her
husband Patrick and surely loved him.

But sadly, tragedies like this happen every day; be it
through illness, accident, or violence. And, like it or not,
the prospect of death for young people increases when
they join the military during a time of war. Not as much,
say, as joining an L.A. street gang and not nearly as much
as cruising the Castro without condoms, but there is no
denying the risk in war, however honorable it be.

And yet Mother Bear continues to blame everyone for
her brave son's death except the evil creeps who killed
him. In fact, she has tried to wash her hands of his joining the Army, saying that she "didn't know he enlisted
until after he phoned and told me." You'd think that such
an important life decision would have been discussed
with a mother who claims to have been so close to her son.

And what did Mother Bear think when her son did
enlist? That the Armed Services was only for people with
upper limbs? "Arms" means weapons. Weapons often lead
to shooting. And shooting often leads to death.

So as tragic as every combat death may be, it shouldn't

come as a surprise. Here are some excerpts from the Oath of Enlistment: *"I swear that I will support and defend the Constitution ... against all enemies, foreign and domestic ... That I will obey the orders of the president of the United States ... So help me God."*

The oath does not say, "I will defend the Constitution against all enemies as long as they promise not to shoot back." Nor does it read, "I will obey the orders of the president as long as they're OK with Mom."

Shame-ham's son, Casey, took this hallowed oath in May 2000 when he enlisted in the U.S. Army—a full sixteen months before a group of cowardly Islamofascists slammed planes into American buildings and soil. Casey took the oath again in August 2003, when he reenlisted at the age of twenty-four, a full six months after we embarked on our liberation of Iraq. Casey was an honor student; he knew what he was doing and what we were doing. He was proud to do it. In fact, his younger sister said soon after his death, "He said he was enjoying the military because it was just like the Boy Scouts, but they got guns."

Two months after Casey's death in April 2004, long before the world had seen the Mother Bear dance, President Bush invited her family and sixteen other grieving families to meet him at Fort Lewis near Seattle.

"We have a lot of respect for the office of the president, and I have a new respect for him because he was sincere and he didn't have to take the time to meet with us," husband Pat told the Sheehans' local California newspaper right after the meeting.

"I now know [the President] is sincere about wanting freedom for the Iraqis," said the Mother Bear herself after their meeting. "I know he's sorry and feels some pain for our loss. And I know he's a man of faith."

The trip also brought the Sheehan family together in a way that none had expected. For a moment, as the local paper reported, life returned to the way it had been before Casey died. The Sheehans and their surviving children laughed and joked as they briefly toured Seattle. They felt whole again.

"That was the gift the president gave us, the gift of happiness, of being together," said Mother Bear.

But then somehow the dancing masters sensed this mother's vulnerability and exploited it. They taught her how to dance the Bush Bash. And bash she did. Just a year after her poignant meeting with the president, she was tanguing to another tune.

When she first met the president, as she now told her new fans, he walked into the room and said callously beyond belief, "Who we all honorin' today?"

"The whole meeting was simply bizarre and disgusting," the Mother Bear claimed of her time with the president, "designed to intimidate instead of providing compassion."

That she could not keep her preposterous stories straight bothered the dancing masters not a whit. Hell's bells, she was a Mother Bear. She had lost a cub. No matter how clumsily she waltzed, no matter whether she forgot her steps, no one could criticize her without looking like a creep.

Heck, Mother Bear could even step on a few toes, even the wrong toes, and the applause still didn't stop. "I think she is a political animal," she said of Senator Hillary Clinton in a takes-one-to-know-one kind of moment. Laying on the animal imagery, Mother Bear accused the good senator of being "a war hawk" just so she could "keep up with the big boys." If the major media overlooked that misstep, they still could not get enough of the Bush Bash. This was the best of all worlds: *American Idol* meets *Animal Planet.*

And even though she's impaired by grief, Mother Bear should have known better than to let her mind be controlled by vermin like George Soros and Steve Bing.

Soros we'll talk about later. But another major contributor to liberal causes like MoveOn—over sixteen million dollars—is the aforementioned Steve "Bling Bling" Bing. To be sure, Bing inherited the bread, some $600 million worth from a grandfather that actually worked for a living, developing luxury buildings in New York in the 1920s.

Once he pocketed his inheritance, Bing dropped out of college to pursue a career in filmmaking. Instead of making films, however, he mostly made film stars. To date, his greatest creative success has been fathering a child with Elizabeth Hurley. Give him credit at least for heterosexuality, an increasingly rare virtue in the Golden State, and for his taste on the Hurley front. But when he tried to avoid the responsibility of financial support with the cavalier quip that "it was her choice to be a single mother," he showed his liberal stripes all too clearly.

This wannabe creative-type has invested his tiny talents and his massive trust fund in teaching the Bush Bash. His chorus line consists of left-footed clodhoppers like Rob Reiner, Warren Beatty, and that PhD of pith, James Caan, who's undergone more body work than a '92 Festiva and hasn't had a good part since Sonny Corleone got whacked thirty-five years ago.

And if you have any doubt that lefties like Soros and Bing weren't behind the world's most celebrated trick bear tour, ask yourself where this middle class mom from Central California is getting the air fare and the smoked salmon.

She's been performing everywhere you look. In Chicago, she danced at the *People's Weekly World* Banquet yes, that *People's Weekly World*, the official organ of the United States Communist Party.

In London, she did her tricks for the Stop the War Coalition and there watched a play about her own life, a story whose script must change daily. After the play, she added a new twist to the Bush Bash, telling these silly Brits,

"Casey was honorable, brave, and sweet, and he was murdered by the Bush family." Oh, those Bushes! Don't they know that America is only supposed to liberate Europeans?

And then a few days later in Ireland, Mother Bear took on Ireland's Foreign Affairs minister for allowing U.S. aircraft to refuel at Shannon Airport. "Your government, even though they didn't send troops to Iraq, are complicit in the crimes by allowing planes to land and refuel." The Irish were sympathetic. The Iraqis aren't ready for democracy, they say, and the country will collapse into civil war. Unlike what? Ireland?

Perhaps the most telling visit she paid was this past January to fellow "peace-activist," Venezuelan Comrade Hugo Chavez, who has sponsored communist terrorist organizations throughout Latin America, and is now reportedly hosting Islamofascist terrorists. Remember, Mother Bear called President Bush "the biggest terrorist in the world today." And what is Chavez? A candidate for this year's Nobel Prize for Political Violence and Regional Terrorism?

Rest assured, the "brutality" Shame-ham suffered by being gently escorted out of the recent State of the Union address in front of the entire Washington press corps is nothing compared to those Venezuelan citizens that have been beaten, stabbed, shot, and murdered in secret by her new dance instructor, Comrade Hugo, and his Latino Gestapo. But I suppose even bears have to dance with the date that escorted them to the party (Communist, in this case).

Repeat a lie often enough, said Lenin, and it becomes the truth. These sentiments didn't come from Mother Bear. The dance masters preyed on her grief and filled her heart with so much bitterness that she Bush Bashed to exorcise the pain. How else to explain such cringe-worthy performances? Remember she did not have to dance well. Her fans were just happy to see her dance at all.

And all the while she did her foolish dance, she cheapened the memory not only of her son, but the memory of hundreds of other sons, who have so bravely died fighting for what this country believes in.

Unfortunately for Sheehan, there are signs that her handlers are looking for a fresher, more attractive and photogenic bear to do their bidding. Once that happens, this pathetic beast will be unceremoniously released from the political zoo and sent back to her original environment, forced to assimilate into what may well be a hostile suburban society.

Be careful out there, Momma Bear. Without the protection of the media and other people's money, it'll be a tough go.

And because of your fifteen minutes of Bush Bashing, America-blaming fame, you've made the go a lot tougher.

George Soros

Leechus omnipotentum

GeoRGe SoRoS

[Leechus omnipotentum]

In the same phylum as the Magyar Maggot, the Budapest Centipede is an insidious invertebrate that has hundreds of hands, all of them out and in other people's business. Although the Budapest Centipede is, of course, native to Hungary ("Buda" is the Magyar word for "lefty," "pest" is the Magyar word for "pest") this particular pest has migrated to the United States where it has become a primary source of energy and resources for native animals of the porno-belts on the East and Left Coasts and native potheads everywhere. Seemingly benign to naive scientists, who often mistake it for a friendly caterpillar, the Budapest Centipede is a voracious parasite that, if not controlled, can pick a hundred pockets simultaneously. As we speak, it is spreading across the country, infesting American homes and eating through their foundations. This small but ambitious bug also travels to the Caribbean, where it has established its own sanctuary, to prevent attacks from the even more predatory insects of the IRS.

George Soros, the poster boy for campaign finance reform who sought single-handedly to buy George Bush out of office, is one of the richest men and biggest pests in America. The Budapest Centipede uses his money to support the concept of an "open society," which he defines as "a society which allows its members the greatest degree of freedom in pursuing their interests compatible with the interests of others." And rest assured, he is putting his money where his mania is, having spent millions of his own just to get reefer legalized under the guise of "medical marijuana." If that succeeds, we will learn what the concept "gateway drug" really means.

For all the libertarian lip, this centipede is a lefty with all hundred of his hands. If you get in the way of this devious vermin, you'll find a hundred knife wounds in your back, "death by a hundred cuts," as the Chinese call it. They know this sucker. Doesn't matter if you're foe or friend. The only person this guy is truly faithful to is Benjamin Franklin.

Remember, this particular breed of centipede comes from the genus Magyar Maggot that spawns in corpses and draws its nourishment from rotting flesh. Britain learned this the hard way. It seems the Budapest Centipede had been hundred-handedly amassing a nest full of English pounds, and on September 6, 1992, a date that's come to be known as Black Wednesday, he sold them short—knowing that it would bollix England's struggling economy. The

Bank of England was forced to devalue the pound sterling, leaving Gorging George with a one-day profit of $1.1 *billion*. For this proto-Democratic effort, Budapest earned the dubious title of "the man who broke the Bank of England." And we're supposed to believe that Republicans are the rich and heartless?

You want a definition of "parasite"? When this bilious billionaire escaped the Soviet occupation of his native Hungary at the age of sixteen, the country that took him in was none other than merry old England, the country that also took in Karl Marx. Didn't they learn? Budapest worked hard and graduated from the London School of Economics where he studied the host country's vulnerabilities long and hard.

And that's how the centipede operates. You let it in to your home, give it warmth, feed it greens, and yet it still starts eating through your floors and your walls until the foundation buckles, the structure comes tumbling down, and the Budapest Centipede worms his way to another host. For the Dems, this pest is pure role model.

Budapest later pulled the same type of maneuvers in both Malaysia and Thailand, where a Thai source said, "We regard him as a kind of Dracula. He sucks blood from people." Yeah, this centipede is a sucker, all right. But you're an even bigger one if you think that he's in this for anyone but himself.

And yet this is a man who once said that his goal was

to earn enough money on Wall Street to support himself as an author and philosopher. Can you imagine what this Kant of cant would say? I can see him now, insider tirading on the steps of the New York Stock Exchange, the left's most prominent economic philosopher since Gordon Gecko got sent upriver. *"Bancito ergo con,"* says Soros, translated "I bank, therefore I scam."

But why even satirize? Here's a bit of real philosophical wit from this pillaging Plato. When asked how he felt about being responsible for so many financial collapses and the number of people devastated by them, Soros said, "As a market participant, I don't need to be concerned with the consequences of my actions."

Such profound wisdom, Kierkegreed. Guess he had to divest his conscience to make room for his money clip. But, alas, this creepy crawling creature hasn't limited his quest for power to foreign shores. No, the centipede has his hundred hands in a hundred different ventures in America's liberal community. Fifty hands giving money to the dopers' bible *Mother Jones* and *The Nation* (a clubby commie chat sheet), as well as the leftwing snakepit MoveOn.org, another fifty hands trying to nitpick the character out of our culture.

In the 2004 U.S. election, of course, Soros became a massive, self-parodying political contributor, saying that removing George Bush from office was the "central focus of my life" as well as being "a matter of life and death." He also claimed he would willingly give up his entire fortune so that George W. Bush would not be reelected.

Well, Bush is still in office and, as far as I can tell, Soros hasn't frequented any soup kitchens lately. But he *did* donate $23,581,000.00 (you read right—over $23 million) to groups opposed to W's return to office. And this from a man who promoted the Bipartisan Campaign Reform Act of 2002, which was intended to ban all "soft money" from federal election campaigns.

But don't be fooled into thinking that his opposition to Bush was based on any philosophical or moral stance. Quite the opposite. You see, in 1986, Soros owned a company called Harken Energy that bought a troubled Texas oil company, Spectrum 7. And who do you think was among the owners of Spectrum 7? If you guessed "Dubya," you win a prize.

But why would the Budapest Centipede make such a seemingly poor business deal? "We were buying political influence," he has said. The problem may have been that he didn't get his money's worth. "It didn't come to anything," he griped.

Unable to buy Bush, the Budapest Centipede has turned instead to buying his opponents. The only problem was that America wasn't buying, at least not in 2004. But make no mistake, the centipede will try again. What this parasite wants has nothing to do with philosophy. It's all about power and control. And what he wants to control is

America. This pest will continue to find ways to funnel funds supporting the campaigns of whatever liberal political puppets will best serve his interests. And once they're in, he'll lead them around like crack addicts hungry for a rock.

What the Budapest Centipede keens for is not mere power for his friends, but a return of the splendor of the Austro-Hungarian empire in which he himself just might make a splendid archduke or, why not, emperor. Heck, why stop there? Soros aspires to divinity. "Let's see," he wonders, "which one of the Trinity is most vulnerable for a buyout?" As this Magyar Maggot actually told *The Observer*, "It is sort of a disease when you consider yourself some kind of god, the creator of everything, but I feel comfortable about it now since I began to live it out."

The Budapest Centipede has his hands in more liberal pies than Jerry Nadler at a dessert buffet. But for all the walking around money a conscienceless hundred-handed creature can pass out, he has yet to worm his way into the heart of America. No wonder the Dems went after Majority Leader Tom DeLay so viciously. It wasn't his history as congressional hammer that scared them. It was his history as a Texas exterminator. He knew what rocks the Budapest Centipede and the other pests were hiding under and wasn't about to ask the EPA if he could spray them out of Washington.

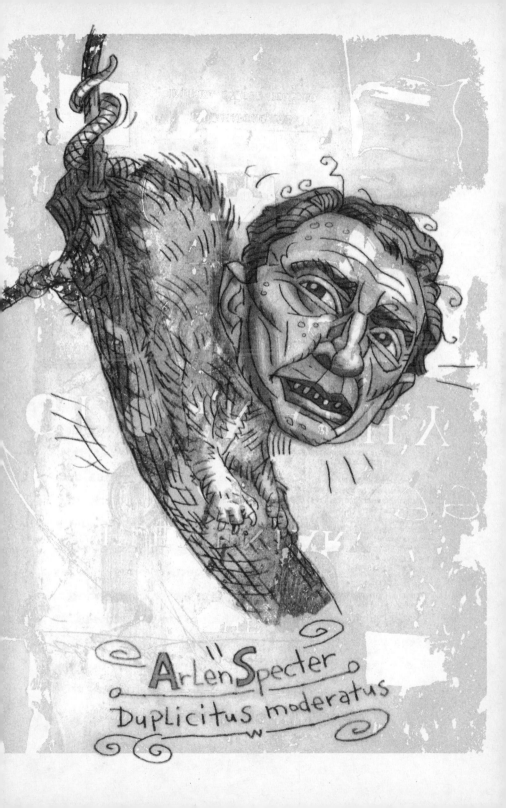

Arlen Specter

Duplicitus moderatus

ARLeN SPeCTeR

[*Duplicitus moderatus*]

The Pennsylvania Scotch Possum is one of the forest's homeliest creatures, known for its pointed snout and equally pointed temper. Every six years, the Scotch Possum goes into hiding. During that time, if it comes across any potential foe, especially within its own species, this marsupial quickly drops to the ground motionless and pretends to be a Republican. If that doesn't work, this crafty creature scampers behind a bush (of the junior variety) to hide its true colors. During the other five and a half years of its lifecycle, this peculiar breed refuses to associate with other possums. Never quite satiated, this omnivorous mammal, which often associates with the equally predatory legal eagles, scavenges through the trash bins and gutters of America's political and legal alleyways and is known to eat fresh meat, crow, and anything green.

How many lawyers does it take to screw in a lightbulb?
I don't know, but it takes only one to screw an entire country. And his name is Arlen Specter. You may recall that while the rest of us labor under American law, this possum operates under Scottish law, which he cited when he voted to acquit President Clinton. "There could be three possible verdicts: guilty, not guilty, not proved," he told a surprised America, and in so saying raised his reputation from middle-of-the-roadness to new comic heights.

The erstwhile Democrat and Warren Commission staff attorney has come a long way from his first heady days of notoriety when he contrived the "single bullet" theory in the JFK assassination. He has now clawed his way to the top of the political pile, today serving as Senate Judiciary Committee chairman. And although he initially ran as a Republican because that was the only way he could get elected as a district attorney, the Scotch Possum currently enjoys the full backing of the GOP president and the official Republican Party.

Of course, the Republican Party has lowered its standards a bit. I suspect Castro could run on the GOP ticket if he had a Bible under his arm, a bowtie around his neck, and a few million in his marsupial pouch.

The playful Scotch Possum has been playing at Republicanism for years. Although one of the most relentless liberals in Congress, he knows enough to feign otherwise—at least when the light is on him. Under the guise of night, however, this creature scavenges through the trash of his civilized betters and consorts with a rogue's galley of left-pawed gutter rats and worse. In 1996, for instance, talk radio slime mold Howard Stern emerged from the slime to endorse his Scotch Possum posse mate in his preposterous bid for the presidency.

And this litigious little critter has never met a lawsuit he didn't like. This has made him an unlikely favorite of America's openly Democrat trial attorneys. In the 2003-2004 election cycle, only the Four Congressmen of the Apocalypse—John Kerry, John Edwards, Joe Lieberman, and Tom Daschle—pocketed more campaign moolah from trial lawyers. Overall, this furry pest got $1.8 million for his reelection campaign from those parasites, his reward for blocking virtually every tort reform package that has gone to the Judiciary Committee since this toothy old possum was first elected as a Whig in that heated campaign of 1836.

Trial lawyers and Howard Stern. Now if only the Ayatollahs would come on board, Specter could get a *New York Times* endorsement, and probably already has.

Of course, the Scotch Possum knows a thing or two about trial lawyering himself. As a defense attorney in private practice when he was first considering a run for the Senate, this marsupial helped to arrange the escape of one of his clients on trial for the murder of his girlfriend, the notoriously unhygienic leftist environmentalist and Earth

Day founder, Ira Einhorn—who wanted to clean up the entire world as long as it didn't include his own under-arms. To get the bail lowered, this devious possum chided the judge that Ira wasn't about to run off to Norway. Ha, ha, ha! The Scotch Possum wasn't lying. Einhorn actually ran away to Sweden, and Specter had rescued another piece of refuse from America's dumpsters.

None of this history, however, prevented Bush, Cheney, and fellow Pennsylvanian Rick Santorum, from backing this weasly little creature in his 2004 reelection primary against a tough conservative willing to fight in the daylight. The conventional wisdom was that having a moderate Republican on the ticket would help Bush in the Keystone State. Despite the heavy guns that were brought out in support of the Scotch Possum, including a presidential fly-in, his primary opponent, Pat Toomey, made it a very close race. When the general election returns came in, it was clear that the Scotch Possum didn't have any coattails for the president to ride on. PA went blue, but apparently Bush carried Glasgow.

Were the election results somehow a surprise to the GOP geniuses that thought up this strategy? What exactly did they make of the "Kerry and Specter for Working Families" campaign posters that appeared all around Pennsylvania?

Were they an attack from Toomey's campaign? No. Was it John Kerry trying to hitch a ride with his fellow senator? Wasn't that either. The signs were created, paid for, and posted by a 527 created by Roger Stone, chairman of Specter's 1996 presidential campaign. How's that for biting the hand that feeds you?

And how did the Scotch Possum reward the president and party's loyalty to help him get reelected? Right after the election, he threatened the White House that he would block any conservative nominees he considered "too extreme," which is basically anyone who doesn't believe the Constitution came with its own bottle of whiteout. After all, it was this ground-hugging creature that doomed Reagan Supreme Court nominee Robert Bork because Bork didn't believe in a "living, breathing" Constitution. "Living and breathing"? The Scotch Possum and his crowd won't be satisfied until the Constitution cross-dresses and sings Judy Garland standards.

And while conservatives, who make up the core of the Republican Party, argue that runaway courts are one of the major problems in American government, Scotch says that they're one of the best answers! That's because this crafty possum, who protects predators like himself, may play Republican when threatened, but the moment one's back is turned, out come the fangs and claws of the predatory Democrat.

Ever since Senate Republicans were duped by this possum's tricks and allowed him to take up the Judiciary Chairmanship, the possum has also become quite the constitutional scholar. When John Roberts came before the committee as a Supreme Court nominee last year, the Scotch Possum unearthed a new term, "superprecedent," to identify legal decisions, like *Roe v. Wade*, which he thinks are so "inviolate" that conservative judges, like Roberts, shouldn't be allowed to even think about them. Where did the Scotch Possum buy his law books? Afghanistan?

Faster than a speed freak lobbyist, more powerful than a loco-pro-lifer, able to leap over the Constitution in a single bound. Is it a word? Is it a shame? Yes, it's a super-precedent!

Aren't we all thrilled that the Constitution and the control of who interprets it are in such capable claws? Aren't we relieved that those same claws capable of burying the assassination of JFK are now employed in the deep-sixing of Able Danger (the once-secret and absolutely necessary intelligence program focused on keeping track of Al Qaeda)? Can't we all sleep better at night?

No, we cannot. For while this possum is sleeping with the Republicans in daytime, he continues to dumpster dive at night with his Democratic soulmates and trial lawyer buddies. And when you dig through the trash, as the Scotch Possum does, you're bound to get dirty.

HoWaRD STeRN

[*Schlocko jocko*]

This colorful, gangly creature is a mutant strain of the Long Island Parrot, or LIP species, bred accidentally on one of the Island's many toxic waste sites. The LIP has an uncanny ability to mimic the most vile comments that it hears and play them back with an added layer of verbal sewage. Preferring to jabber only early in the morning, the LIP spends the rest of its day scavenging the New York City waste system for new tidbits to repeat for its next morning's appearance. Although this sewer spewer boasts that he cannot be tamed, his vision is impaired to the fact that he is the favorite pet of global media monkeys, who quietly program his every spontaneous syllable.

Because Howard Stern has jumped ship from the public airwaves and gone to the extraterrestrial world of satellite radio, we mere earthlings can breathe a lot easier. We don't have to worry about our kids stumbling across this foul fowl while station surfing in the old SUV.

Some bird watchers have reported that this mutant bird is featherless. It is alleged that his mane is a wig; that beneath it all, without the hairpiece, Stern looks like a dentist from the Bronx (circa 1945), who sells condoms on the side. Others compare him to the "balloon men" once known to Catskill Mountain bungalow colonies. Lowlifes who came around in broken cars to entertain the uneducated summer renters with balloons they twisted into the forms of animals performing obscene acts.

But even if he is a featherless freak, you have to give the Long Island Parrot (LIP) credit for keeping an audience for the past twenty years by making obscene sounds from either end of its plumed body into a microphone.

His biggest draw is ridiculing mentally handicapped people, an act that should be a federal crime, violating the civil rights of those too incapacitated to know they're being picked on. Some find this funny. Others wonder why the federal government doesn't arrest this verminous slug and charge him with a hate crime for using the handicapped for sport. Still others fear he is the embodiment of the worst "entertainment" since the

Weimar Republic and that he might bring about a new Hitler-like reaction.

Bird watchers have also observed that the LIP is "evolving," never a good thing. This one-time politically incorrect bad boy (and closet Republican) gave up his street smarts for stupid sex when he first went national. By the time of his first foray into politics in 1994, he was running for governor of New York on the Libertarian ticket. Urban issues fell by the wayside—and his marriage would soon follow—as he focused on such things as legalized prostitution, lesbian coupling, and same-sex marriage. He even promised free sex, apparently a concept his wife wasn't keen on. But when his campaign picked up a modicum of steam, this self-serving provocateur withdrew from the race for refusing to disclose his income in accordance with election laws.

Guess this zero had too many questionable zeroes.

And who can forget his famous promise of the 2004 election, when a poll conducted by the New York Democratic Network estimated that 4 percent of undecided likely voters were Stern listeners. So what did the LIP do? He parroted the line of his new Left Coast buddies and urged his fans to vote for the dreary John Kerry.

And why this sudden love of Kerry? Sad to say, even though the LIP had previously supported Bush, he changed his so-called allegiance after reading a book by none other than the philosopher king of *Saturday Night Live*, Stuart Smalley.

Using Al Franken-stooge's book to guide you politically is like asking Martha Stewart to guide you on ethical investment strategies.

So what happened to the Long Island Parrot's electoral wave? It crashed on the rocks of political reality. The Bling of All Media vastly overestimated the political impact of his show. He forgot that most of those fans were too wasted to register, let alone vote. And don't ever frustrate them with a butterfly ballot!

Now that the LIP is on satellite radio, we can be spared the regular ritual of Stern trumpeting his constant harassment and persecution by the dreaded FCC, one of the most spineless agencies of the federal government. Long known to be at the beck and call of entertainment conglomerates, the FCC has about as much power as a Yugo going up a hill.

So what was the FCC controversy all about? Wake up and smell the con, folks! The LIP's bosses wanted those fines: they begged for those fines, they had the LIP do all the vile cackling and chattering he could do—including Rosie O'Donnell imitations—to guarantee those fines. The FCC's pusillanimous bit of persecution is what made the LIP and his bad boy reputation.

The truth is that the FCC attacks were all part of the

station's corporate marketing strategy. What's a few million bucks to bolster sagging ratings to media companies
that would rake in ten times that amount in additional ad
revenues? In the Long Island Parrot's world, is there any
such thing as bad publicity? No, remember, the LIP comes
from the same slice of real estate that produced Joey
Buttofuoco and the Long Island Lolita, Amy Fisher (no
joke, a televised reunion is in the works). The LIP's antics
were bought and paid for by his media puppeteers.

And all this was disguised as a principle of "Free
Speech," two words that he has learned to repeat as if
they had real meaning, and James Madison's worst nightmare come to life.

And yet, people are still taken in by this skilled
mimic's masterful media manipulation. In fact, an article
in the *UK Guardian* went so far as to call him the "Last
Defender of Freedom." Quick, get the air-sickness bag.

If that's the case, we're in a huge pile of trouble, unless
we study how "independent" this Defender of Freedom
was while he was on the air?

It seems the LIP has a curious definition of free speech.
Did you ever wonder why the irreverent and unfunny LIP
wannabes from the *Opie & Anthony Show* suddenly
stopped their relentless mocking of him on the air?

The quiet truth is that both radio programs aired on
Infinity Broadcasting, a network that counted on its

favorite parrot to generate ad revenue. So the LIP used his leverage with Infinity's parent company, Viacom, to get Opie and Anthony to stop talking smack about him. In fact, he pressured Viacom to prohibit them from even mentioning his name on their show. I wonder if he learned that from reading Al "Machiavelli" Franken. That's the kind of free speech that even Hugo Chavez could understand. Can a Venezuela visit be far away for this leftward sliding sham libertarian?

But the LIP isn't the only one who is flocking to the unregulated skies of satellite radio. Guess who is now on XM Satellite Radio, Sirius' larger competitor? Stern's old friends of a feather, Opie and Anthony. And there's no Infinity Broadcasting to protect the parrot anymore.

Because of these two new parrot predators flying around Stern's satellite skies, the LIP pulled his twenty-two-year-old daughter, Emily, from an off-Broadway nude review (what used to be called strip clubs) to prevent Opie and Anthony fans from showing up to take pictures to embarrass the Papa Parrot. Freedom of speech and expression is only allowed in his birdcage, and exploiting strippers is only for other families' daughters, it seems.

Looks like Polly can dish it out, but can't take it.

As the LIP has likely learned already, his recent move to Sirius satellite radio will hasten his slide even further into broadcasting irrelevancy. Foul-mouthed parrots, after all, gain attention only by repeating their vile imprecations in the presence of people who can be offended. On satellite, unless there are space aliens listening in, the LIP will have no one to offend.

In fact, it is likely that he will disappoint his Sirius fans by not being vile enough. These are kids who breakfast each morning on quadruple X pornography. What can the LIP repeat that they have not heard a thousand times already and done a hundred?

And you can count on this self-proclaimed libertarian to get a harsh lesson in free market economics when he learns that most of his listeners won't be willing to dip into their Jaegermeister funds to pay for what they used to get for free.

It won't be long before a new sophomoric sensationalist will come along and invariably take over where the flapped-out old LIP left off. This new wonder parrot will have mimicked the chatter in dives too gross for even the LIP, and our veteran low-flying LIP will surely be clipped by a lower flying one.

And that's the way the culture coarsens.

Barbra Streisand
Bovine fundraisium

BARBRA STREiSaND

[Bovine fundraisium]

The Streisand Cow is an over-aged, overfed, and often-milked cash cow that plods around her pen, sagging and swaying with every lumbering move she makes. Once known for her ability to make beautiful sounds, this hefty Bessie now stuffs that same mouth with Big Macs when not spouting boorish, bovine, left-hoof nonsense. Although most species are smart enough to sidestep her ample, over-ripe droppings, those foolish to stick their snouts in have all too often been infected with potentially lethal cases of the Rad Cow Disease that long ago stole this bovine's good sense.

345

Barbra Streisand, the Rad Cow of California, is the perfect barnyard partner for the voracious Democratic Jackass. She feeds millions in fundraising moo-lah into the Democratic trough every year. In reward for her labors, the jackasses have allowed her to bray for their causes as their self-proclaimed Left Coast intellectual.

Barbra Streisand? Intellectual?

Yes, intellectual, but only in that part of the world where Iran-mullah-supporting Sean Penn can pass for a pacifist, Kaballah-babbling Madonna can pass for a religious Jewish scholar of mysticism, and Rock Hudson could pass for a man's man.

I guess there's something about having a diploma from an accredited high school and the charm of a frumpy school marm that empowers the Rad Cow to speak out on subjects about which she knows nothing, which is just about everything.

But notice that she always releases her free-ranging opinions either through one-on-one interviews or on her website. Why? Because the Rad Cow says she suffers from glossophobia, which is the fear of speaking in front of large herds. We'd all be a lot better off if she could just develop Bossy-phobia, which is the fear of sounding like a cow's udder at dawn.

Consider just a few of the moo-sings from a female who considers herself something of a barnyard authority on so many things: On her website, she restated her "deep opposition to the Iranian dictator, Saddam Hussein."

Oh, well . . . *Iran, Iraq. Tomato, Tomahto.* What's the diff?

Shortly thereafter, the Rad Cow claimed that President Bush was pushing for war in Iraq because of his deep ties to the logging industry. That's right, *logging.* I guess only God and Babsie know how much we rely on Baghdad birch to build those gaudy Malibu mansions.

And yet, despite her contributions to the cause, when her good pal Billy Bob Clinton was president, he invited Sharon Stone—and not her—to the White House for consultation. The Rad Cow was heard to bellow, "Why Sharon Stone? What does *she* know about policy?"

Not much, I imagine. But I'm male enough to know the difference between a cow and a fox, and I suspect that the Wolf in the White House did as well. Let's see. Who would a red-blooded male of any species rather spend an Oral Office afternoon with: Barbra Streisand or Sharon Stone? Hmmmm, let's see . . . Sharon Stone is certainly prettier, usually wittier, and as yet, slightly more resistant to gravity in certain critical places.

Tough decision.

OK, this Malibu Milk Dud may not be as constitutionally perky as Ms. Stone, but she does know her First Amendment. You know, freedom of speech, expression, etc.

The Rad Cow absolutely believes in a free press, at least as long as the "free" press agrees with her, and that has not happened since *Pravda* privatized. Even the left-leaning *Los Angeles Times* irks her because it does not lean left enough. In fact, she cancelled her subscription because she thought the paper too conservative. The *Los Angeles Times* too conservative? Right. And Elton John is too macho.

And what offense did the *Times* commit to dry up this cash cow's $4.50 a month? The paper had the nerve not to renew the contract of Robert Scheer, a blue state op-ed pinko. This is the same Robert Scheer who had previously abandoned his journalistic integrity to advise the Rad Cow on a speech she was making at Harvard—Harvard "Yard" actually, a less threatening environment for a bovine glossophobe.

This is also the same Robert Scheer for whom the Rad Cow threw a party to celebrate the release of his most recent Bush-bashing tome.

Streisand doesn't so much want freedom *of* speech as freedom *from* speech. Public or private, speech isn't her strong suit. In her letter to the *Times* announcing her subscription cancellation, she decried the paper's lack of the "princi*pals* of journalistic integrity." Right, what does anyone in Malibu know about princi*ples*?

And then there's her mewling about CBS's decision to move its misbegotten mini-series about President Ronald Reagan from network to cable. This was her husband playing the Gipper! No, not Elliot Gould, but James Brolin-

Streisand, the former Meineke spokesman who's hawked more mufflers than a Times Square scarf peddler.

This is the same CBS, by the way, that the Rad Cow once praised for Dan Rather's misreporting on President Bush's military record. You remember the story that soon proved to be, in Rather's memorable oxymoron, "fake but accurate."

Perhaps Ms. Streisand's finest First Amendment hour came when she sued the California Coastal Records Project for taking an aerial picture of her Malibu mansion, which sits on a knoll above the Pacific. According to environmental experts, her ten-thousand-square-foot Baghdad birch "cottage" and surrounding pasturage have been responsible for significant coastline erosion in the area.

The random showing of an aerial photograph of her house, which was one of twelve thousand frames taken of the California coastline, so twisted her udder that she sued the photographer/founder of the agency for fifty million dollars, claiming invasion of privacy.

"I don't want everyone to see me grazing" she allegedly said. No, she didn't really say that. But she did say, "I don't want everyone to see how I arrange my lawn furniture." Almost as bad. Perhaps she hoped to recycle the fifty million dollars—minus legal fees—back into her favorite environmental causes.

Ironically, the right to free expression falls under the

same general legal protection as freedom of speech, and the judge decided that the Left Coast Freedom Fighter was not on the right side of this one. He dismissed her case and ordered her to pay $155,567.04 for the defendant's legal fees.

$155,567.04. That'd buy a lot of feed grain. Of course, it was just a drop in the milk bucket for this chronic complainer about things that don't go her way.

Perhaps instead of exercising her First Amendment right to free speech, she should invoke her Fifth Amendment right to keep silent. That way she would avoid getting taken to the slaughterhouse every time she steps in her own verbal cow paddies. In a speech at the 2002 Democratic National Gala, she quoted a passage that she attributed to Shakespeare's *Julius Caesar* to attack the Bush administration and the War in Iraq. Except the quote wasn't by Shakespeare. One professor of English, a world-renowned Shakespeare expert, spoke for the entire free world when he commented on bovine Barb's Bard bastardization by saying, "Only an artistic imbecile would fall for that pathetic quote being Shakespeare. Streisand is a lame-brained sucker. What a dope!" The Bard himself couldn't have said it better!

Her response to the fact-checking fiasco was straight out of Dan Rather's playbook. "The authorship of this is important, but it doesn't detract from the fact that the words themselves are powerful and true and beautifully written." So frequent are her verbal gaffes that she has an entire section of her website devoted to the Orwellian-named "Truth Archive" to correct her many mistakes.

It seems that even Malibu malcontents are growing weary of her constant mooing and missteps. Maybe they're just tired of having her represent all the cattle in the herd. On the set of *Meet the Fockers*, in which she portrayed a sex therapist (yikes —one session with her could cure me of ever wanting sex), a producer had the audacity to call her "Barb." She snapped at him and made it clear that this wasn't a nickname she appreciated.

Well, uber liberal co-star Dustin Hoffman reportedly heard this exchange and began calling her "Barb" as well. And if this weren't enough to get under the hide of this pampered pain, imagine her shock when she showed up at the set to find the entire film crew wearing "Bush/Cheney 2004" buttons. When she found out that Hoffman was behind the prank, she stormed off the set!

I guess to this ambling bloviator, freedom of speech can only be so free. The Rad Cow undoubtedly remains in the zoo, making rare appearances for the public. But do not feed her; she's packed away enough to last for many a winter. And should you get too close, be careful where you step. Rad Cow disease is infectious, especially among the young, the tan, and the simple-minded.

Arthur Sulzberger
Silverus spoohus

ARTHuR SuLZ BeRGeR JR.

[*Silverus spoonus*]

Even for a poodle, the Pampered Pinch Poodle is remarkably untalented. The only trick he can do is bark, and that he does neither loud nor convincingly. Were it not for his extraordinary pedigree, no one would pay this dog any mind. Lacking any known skill, the Pinch Poodle relies on a long tradition of inbreeding, exquisite grooming, and old-fashioned nepotism for his elevated status in the Political Zoo. And although fully grown, he still insists on leaving his droppings on newspapers. Thankfully, his favorite mats are the *New York Times* and *the Boston Globe*.

Arthur "Pinch" Sulzberger Jr., or "Pinchy" as I call him, is the chairman of the New York Times Company and publisher of the *New York Times*. He inherited this position in 1992 at the age of forty-one from his father, Arthur "Punch" Sulzberger Sr., who had to have been punchy to turn the *Times* over to Pinchy.

Surely one who would rise so quickly must have amazing credentials. Yes and no. Following in the footsteps of Roadrunner Bill Richardson, Pinchy graduated from Tufts University, an obvious dumping ground for pups with more pedigree than tricks. The school's sports teams call themselves the "Jumbos," which suggests that even they don't take themselves seriously. A political science major, Pinchy landed a job as a reporter for the Raleigh, North Carolina *Times* after graduation. Strictly on his own talents, of course.

Following two exciting years covering stories like North Carolina State basketball and the rising price of tar, this pup reporter was lured away by the Associated Press. His talent showed itself quickly once again, and after two more years, the *New York Times* found him meaningful work in its Washington bureau.

For the record, the Pinchy's great grandpa bought the *Times* in 1896. And then, he turned it over to Granddaddy Doggie in 1935, who passed it on to "Punch," or P-Daddy as he is known, in 1961.

Amazingly, with no degree in journalism and only four

years after graduation, Pinchy managed to overcome the obstacles and land a job at the *New York Times*. Bow-Wow! Only sham artist Jayson Blair moved to and through the *Times* that quickly, and Blair did his without even a college degree.

In the not too distant past—prior to Prince Pinchy's ascending the poodle throne—the *New York Times* was a beacon that put fairness above all. Oh, it was liberal, all right. What in New York wasn't? But before Pinchy's leadership, the *Times* tried to balance both its reporting and its editorials with opposing points of view. Retired *Boston Globe* columnist David Warsh said in 2003 that under the leadership of P-Daddy, the editors "managed to keep the paper both balanced and enterprising. Fair play is harder than it looks."

Under Pinchy, says Warsh, the paper's "dominant overtones seem, at least to me, to have become strident, intemperate, even undignified."

Pinchy went ahead and bought the *Boston Globe*. But get this: That was the same year that Pinchy cut the *NY Times'* workforce by ten percent to save money. They don't call this pup "Pinchy" for nothing.

Under Pinchy's dogged leadership, even insiders admit, the *Times* has become an easy access soapbox for every lefty with a sob story or a gripe. Now you'd think that a paper that boasts that it is "fair and balanced" would deny such a claim. But sometimes the truth sneaks out. When asked about the paper's political slant, temporary public editor Daniel Okrent wrote that the *Times* is "of course" a liberal newspaper.

And listen to what the Poodle Publisher barked to the Associated Press in a 2003 interview. Referring to the *Times*, he said, "We are enormously powerful, and we are very scary."

Scary, for sure. And here's just one of the reasons why. When the Pinch was still a pup, during the height of Vietnam, his father asked him, "If an American soldier runs into a North Vietnamese soldier, which would you like to see get shot?"

"I would want to see the American get shot," he said. "It's the other guy's country." He didn't seem to care—or even know—that our enemies were North Vietnamese, who were not fighting in their country. The South was about as much a part of the North as France was a part of Germany on D-Day. Ask the Germans. Talk about a patriot.

So is it any wonder why the paper is so anti-Iraq War with poodle-head at the helm? Said Gay Talese, author of the definitive history of the *Times*, *The Kingdom and the Power*, "You get a bad king every once in a while."

Now if Saddam had been torturing and murdering gays—and we don't mean Mr. Talese—instead of mere Iraqis it would have been a different story. This proud Outward Bound graduate might have led his own poodle platoon.

Being a poodle, however straight, Pinch has taken a special interest in gays. When he took over the paper, he reportedly took every gay on the staff to lunch individually and promised to make the newspaper the most gay-friendly newspaper in the country. At this project, by all accounts, he has succeeded. The paper may be tanking, but the cubicles are the best decorated in the industry.

Now there are a lot of folks who will say that every paper is biased one way or the other. Maybe. Maybe not. But either way, the accuracy of individual newspapers is generally accepted.

Not so fast, *New York Times.*

Look at just a few of the hugely embarrassing incidents of false and misleading reporting that have occurred under Junior's watch.

In the run up to the 2003 Masters Golf Tournament, then editor Howell Raines launched a one-paper campaign to force these spoiled rich guys at Augusta National to accept equally spoiled rich women into their club. You can imagine how this noble cause resonated throughout the dog pounds of America. To its credit, Augusta National stood its ground, and no matter how Pinchy and his poodle friends huffed and puffed, they couldn't convince anyone they were wolves.

Then, too, there was the debacle of Jayson Blair, the coked-up reporter who imagined cows in Jessica Lynch's front yard from his apartment in Brooklyn. Like the Pinch, he too was fast-tracked into his position, in Blair's case because Pinchy had initiated a policy that froze the hiring of non-black male heterosexuals and, according to one *Times* veteran, "set up an unofficial little quota system."

In 2003, Blair was nabbed plagiarizing a news story, and a further internal investigation revealed that there were at least thirty-six other stories that Blair wrote that contained more instances of plagiarism, mistruths, or bald-faced lies. All this from a publication that claims to be "America's newspaper of record."

Pinchy had his nose rubbed in the mess he made by an opportunistic media and an angered populace. When asked what he thought about the scandal, Pinchy growled, "It sucks." Remember, this is not a brooding, nose-pierced fifteen-year-old bass guitarist, but the head of the most influential newspaper in the world.

Although now in his mid-fifties, Pinchy still has a serious case of GD, gravitas deficiency. This manifested itself big time when he insisted on meeting jailed reporter Judith Miller on her departure from prison. Miller had served nearly three months for protecting source Scooter Libby in the Plamegate affair. Apparently, Pinch scampered friskily up to the tinted-glass vehicle in which the marshals were transporting Miller and tapped puppy-like at the window, saying, "Judy! It's me." The marshals told him in no uncertain terms to scoot, and he did. So did Miller. Within months, she was canned essentially for reporting what every intelligence service in the world knew to be true, namely that Saddam had WMDs. Apparently, Frank Rich and Maureen Dowd knew better.

Because of readers' lack of trust, the *Times'* stock price is in free fall, dropping 1/3 just in the year 2005. All newspapers are at risk, but the *Times* is falling 60 percent faster than the industry norm. A senior *Times* corporate executive told the *New Yorker* magazine, "It's just a matter of time until we start losing money."

So the next time you peruse the pages of this rag, even in cyberspace, remember what your loyal zookeeper has told you. If you see an article protesting the NSA's taping phone calls of Al Qaeda's Islamofascist operatives in the United States, or a separate piece screaming for the scalp of Karl Rove for the outing of the CIA desk jockey Valerie Plame, consider the source.

I grew up in New York. In my younger days, I read the *Times* cover to cover, taking in both sides of a story. But P-Daddy is long gone, and the Pinch Puppy is now pooping on the press. One of the world's great newspapers has now no greater purpose than to push the angry Left's prosaic diatribes.

Donald Trump

Mondo condo convertus

DoNaLD TRUMP

[*Mondo condoconvertus*]

The Great American Balding Eagle, which can be seen flying high above New York City, has become synonymous with the gaudy architecture and over-priced luxury housing where it perches. The Balding Eagle is an overly ambitious and productive creature, with a mouth as vast as its wingspan, both of which ceaselessly flap. This bird has found a new habitat on the airwaves, the peacock network as would seem appropriate. Here, in this electronic version of nature tooth and claw, the Balding Eagle tests the Darwinian skills of various animals and, at show's end, eats the loser. He also eats fish, birds, small mammals, and unwary creditors. Although most of this species are monogamous, the Balding Eagle hunts down foreign creatures to mate with, at least until its mate ages, and then roosts elsewhere.

In the eerie convergence of pop culture and personality driven politics, no suggestion is more startling about a move into the political world than that of Donald Trump, America's favorite financier. A predatory bird, who's had a bad hair day for the last 21,000 straight, this less-than-regal eagle has allowed the speculation to run rampant about his throwing his reported rug into the political ring. In 2000, he made an actual stab at the Reform Party presidential nomination. Recently he's been talked up by some New York politicians about running for governor—a report he has softly denied on his blog. Yes, the Balding Eagle is such a tease.

Of course, Trump has no discernible political philosophy, contributing money to both the Republican and Democratic Parties, keeping all of his nests covered. So when the Balding Eagle talks politics, it is usually nothing more than a hodge-podge of socialist economics and soft-core cultural Trotskyism—like his plan to tax the super-rich (those with ten million dollars or more in assets) at a 14.75 rate on a one-time basis to pay off the national debt. Can we really take seriously a plan to eliminate the national debt from a man that has dealt with his own massive corporate debts through bankruptcy court? Maybe President Trump would put the U.S. into Chapter 13.

Some have even described the Balding Eagle as a libertarian. However, this predatory creature loves public power. At least once, he had his fellow predators in

Atlantic City use eminent domain to snatch and raze the home of a retired widow to make room for more limousine parking at his casino. How much more libertarian can you get than that?

And you have to wonder what his campaign platform would look like. Slot machines in every home instead of taxation? Kids who get to fire their parents if they fall below a certain income?

Maybe this guy does have the brains to succeed in politics. I mean, this big bird loves the camera, even if the camera doesn't reciprocate. He has enough charisma (or "chi") to push even Chuck Schumer away from the lens. Can you imagine this guy on the campaign trail? He's a bigger self-promoter than P.T. Barnum. I could even see him, once elected, introducing legislation to create a new T-Span channel devoted exclusively to Trump himself 24/7.

And the Balding Eagle certainly understands the political way of handling public funds. In the spirit of former Senator Everett Dirksen, who once famously quipped, "A billion here and a billion there, and soon you're talking about real money," Trump has likewise described how he conducts business: "When I build something for somebody, I always add $50 million or $60 million onto the price. My guys come in, they say it's going to cost $75 million. I say it's going to cost $125 million, and I build it for $100 million. Basically, I did a lousy job. But they think I did a great job."

Sounds like this bird of prey would be a perfect fit for Congress.

The presidency, however, would be more Trump's style. He could put a big, gaudy gold metallic "Trump" sign on top of the White House, which would then be renamed Trump House. The one dollar bill would have to be redesigned with the country's new motto, "In Trump We Trust," and the Bald Eagle would be replaced with a picture of the Balding Eagle clutching hairspray and a comb.

And if his longstanding beef with billionaire Mark Cuban is any indication of his diplomatic skills, don't look for The Donald to be nominated as secretary of state or U.N. ambassador anytime soon. The two started fighting when Cuban's not quite as successful rival program, *The Benefactor*, was going head-to-head with *The Apprentice*. When Cuban's show was cancelled, Trump sent him a memo gloating over its demise. Well, Donald, Vladimir Putin probably won't like it when you rub it in his face that we were able to invade Afghanistan when the Russians couldn't. Pissing off people with nuclear weapons is a little more dangerous than someone with an NBA team.

While he waits for his ambassadorial appointment, Trump plans to sharpen his diplomatic skills by offering to help President Bush in dealing with the Saudis over high gasoline prices. "Stop sending those politicians over there to negotiate," he recently complained on his blog. "A seasoned business negotiator could do some serious talking, and those prices would drop like a rock." He might soon learn that when it comes to foreign policy, not everyone plays by the eagle's rules, no matter how close he builds his nest to U.N. Headquarters. Instead of hearing "You're fired," Trump might hear shouts of "Allah Akbar," before having his comb over lopped off on live TV by black-hooded barbers.

Instead of taking those kind of risks, maybe the Balding Eagle can help America by leading the next wave of election reform, reality TV-style. He has said, "One of the key problems today is that politics is such a disgrace, good people don't go into government." Perhaps instead of elections, candidates for public office in the future will be placed on a Trump-hosted political version of *The Apprentice*. And in place of political parties, contestants will be divided into "Book Smarts" and "Street Smarts" teams.

And just to add a democratic element to the show, maybe Randy, Paula, and Simon of *American Idol* can make the initial cuts and save us all that primary hassle. Voters would call 1-800 numbers each week—one for English, two for Spanish—to vote for their preferred candidates. Results could be announced the following day on a special two-hour election results show where all the candidates could perform before America is told who gets cut from the election.

Another political reform the Balding Eagle could run on comes straight out of his personal life. One of Trump's most famous maxims—one he practices as well as preaches—is "always have a pre-nup." Maybe instead of relying on the cumbersome impeachment process, as costly and bitter as a divorce, all elected officials would have to sign a pre-nup with voters to dissolve the relationship if the office doesn't work out. And they lose their pensions! The Balding Eagle could be the first to sign. Even if impeached, it wouldn't cost near what it did to dump Ivana and Marla.

But although the eagle is one of nature's great predators, there is little to fear from this Gotham bird, building towering gold-plated nests to house his many golden eggs in Washington or Albany. It would be hard for him to fly the coop from his Manhattan perch.

And you really have to wonder how well Trump would take to politics with the Balding Eagle's thin skin. Having to constantly face down a hostile press corps, Trump would no longer be able to sue reporters for unflattering stories, like he did earlier this year when he sued a *New York Times* business reporter for $5 billion (at least he uses enough zeroes to be a politician) for daring to claim that his net worth is really around $250 million, instead of the $2.7 billion he claims. Of course, appearing so desperate for cash doesn't help this legal eagle's case. Despite his protestations to the contrary, the Balding Eagle seems to be less lucky in lucre than meets an eagle eye.

Yes, it might be a while before America tells Trump, "You're hired!"

Ted Turner
Mouthus desouthus

TED TURNeR

[*Mouthus desouthus*]

The Southern Widemouth Copperhead is an unpredictable, aggressive reptile that is adept at moving into new areas and exerting territorial dominance. Its preferred method of attack is to open its enormous, venom-laden jaws and strike. But it is at this moment that the Widemouth Copperhead is most vulnerable as it has a tendency to bite itself in the tail. This species was originally contained to Central Georgia, but its habitat now includes vast swaths of New Mexico, Colorado, and Montana. Its irregular mating habits consist of slinking from female to female, who, once caught in his jaws, are never quite sure whether they are amatory interests or prey. The natural enemy for the Widemouth Copperhead is the Murdoch Mongoose, from the snake's perspective, "the most dangerous man in the world."

Billionaire. Media mogul. Cable news pioneer. Sports team owner. Philanthropist. Bigot. Psychotic. Madman. Traitor. Loudmouth. Environmentalist. Buffalo Killer. All of these are accurate descriptions of the "Mouth of the South," Ted "Widemouth" Turner. He coils at your feet, strikes at your face, and spits venom like a viper.

After a lengthy period of study, acclaimed herpetologist Dr. Savage has made the highly specific neurodiagnosis that this snake is just plain nuts. The Widemouth Copperhead cavorts with dictators, defends America's enemies, and insults the country and its citizens, whom he calls "some of the dumbest people in the world." He does this while soaking his incalculable wealth from these very people, a trick that has gotten Turner his photo in the dictionary next to the entry, "Wall Street socialist."

From his launch of the first nationwide cable channel, TBS, to his introduction of CNN the world over, the Widemouth Copperhead has had this Alexander-like urge to conquer. It doesn't matter whether it's sailing or business or baseball or real estate or romance, Ted Turner wants the best and biggest toys at the end of the day.

This voracious reptilian appetite has made him the largest landowner in America. Turner owns some two million acres in seven states, very nearly the size of Rhode Island and Delaware combined, a lot of land for a one-worlder socialist wannabe. But two million acres in the U.S. just wasn't enough for the Widemouth Copperhead; he has now started buying up parts of Argentina to enlarge his ego—excuse me—empire. Besides, if you were married to Jane Fonda, as he once was, you would want to be able to put a little distance between you and her too. Imagine sharing a small apartment with the barbs of Barbarella. His delusions—excuse me again—visions of grandeur also include his mammoth buffalo herds of some forty thousand head, once again the largest in the world. (Is anybody else picking up a theme here? Is the copperhead overcompensating for being such an old and shriveled little snake?)

Of course, having the best toys does not mean you have the best brains to use them. Proof of the same is the Widemouth Copperhead's recent visit to North Korea to discuss his proposal for turning the demilitarized zone into a nature preserve.

Once back home, Turner channeled the spirit of the late, great Soviet suck-up, the *New York Times'* very own Walter Duranty, and claimed that the North Koreans wanted to treat the world as nicely as they treat their own citizens. "I saw a lot of people over there," said Kim Jong-Il's most useful idiot. "They were thin and they were riding bicycles instead of driving in cars, but I didn't see any brutality."

No political oppression there either. He quizzed his assigned government minders, and like Death Camp colonels, they assured him that their guests were happy and healthy. The rumors of widespread starvation were untrue. Their own big bellies were proof of that.

Not surprising for a lefty wannabe, the Widemouth Copperhead also lauds Cuba's Fidel Castro as "one hell of a guy." Doesn't everyone? Fidel's credentials demand respect. No sooner did he and his comrades take over that benighted island than they started seizing property, shutting down newspapers, driving priests into exile, forcing the judiciary to its knees, and organizing an in-your-face intelligence service, a kind of neighborhood NSA. From a liberal perspective, what's not to love? True, the Fidelistos savagely oppressed homosexuals, but they did so mostly before gays were in fashion. Besides, Fidel and friends did so much good, especially the weeding out of capitalist roaders, that a little gay (and straight) bashing is understandable. In that first decade, ten thousand counterrevolutionaries died from shock brought on by the sudden impact of bullets against their chest. Thirty thousand more rotted in prison, and several hundred thousand more fled at great risk in open boats. "One hell of a guy"? Pass the cigars.

It used to be that his ex-wife Jane Fonda was the one giving aid and comfort to America's enemies. But today, it seems there's hardly a totalitarian regime that this snake in the grass isn't slithering up to. I think he appreciates their management style. After a visit with Fidel, the copperhead opened his wide mouth and said, "Castro's not a communist. He's like me—a dictator." That's right Ted, he's also a decrepit, increasingly irrelevant power-mad reptile—just like you.

And don't forget CNN's long-standing propaganda partnership with Saddam Hussein. The unprecedented access that CNN had in Baghdad during the 1991 Gulf War pushed CNN into the cable news stratosphere. CNN became Saddam's preferred outlet for Arab anti-Americanism. But then the dirty secret emerged in 2003. CNN's chief news executive revealed that CNN had to suppress stories of Saddam's violence—including the murder and dismemberment of a CNN news source—to maintain its insider status. U.S. military officials uncovered the incriminating evidence themselves in the Iraqi government's files. I guess that's what you call pay for play.

The Widemouth Copperhead is also well skilled in throwing his money around, if you're just talking heft and not direction. In 1998, he pledged one billion dollars to the United Nations when the Republican-controlled Congress balked at forking over more dues without any reform. As a result, the UN is increasingly funded by private foundations to support programs that America refuses to fund. Thanks, Ted. Better you than the taxpayers.

Turner's favorite UN cause is population control, and he supports programs that force women to undergo abortions and sterilizations. Strange for a man that has had three wives and has five children. At least he's learned to live with his contradictions as every good eugenicist must.

The Widemouth Copperhead reveals his hypocrisy when he speaks of rival news king, Fox News, as an arm of the Bush administration. Worse, he compares its popularity to Hitler's before World War II. Never mind that Turner and the Crescent News Network are in active cahoots with most of the fascist regimes in the world.

You have to forgive this reptile for presenting situations in the starkest terms possible. When he lectured reporters at the National Press Club in 1994 on the barbaric practice of female circumcision, he did so only to compare its victims to himself. "I'm being clitorized by Time-Warner," he said with stupefying insensitivity, "and I don't like it anymore than [Arab women] do." I'm sure they feel your pain, Ted.

Speaking of women, the Widemouth Copperhead gets to play the snake in his own Garden of Eden, forever cooing and cajoling and promising great perks. Bob Hope admitted astonishment at the "incredible number of women Turner ran through," adding, "He was brash, chauvinistic, right to the point. He'd win 'em over and shack 'em up. Then move right on to the next one."

Of course, his not so coy advances don't always work out. Once at a party in New York, Eveready Teddy coiled up next to CNN vice president Mary Alice Williams. Dispensing with all the usual pickup lines, he just clutched her crotch. She was equally direct. She decked him.

Needless to say, his wives have noticed such things and objected. So relentless was this hedonism that he even drove sex kitten Jane Fonda into the arms of Christianity, "a religion for losers," in the Widemouth Copperhead's estimate.

No, in his paradise there was room for only one power source and that was his very own serpentine self. The snake was beside himself when Ms. Fonda announced her conversion. Turner's eldest daughter, Laura, traces his problem with his wife's embrace of Jesus to a very basic drive: "It was another male," she says. "It took time away from him."